The cover picture is the face of Christ from the conch of the apse of the Cathedral at Cefalu, Sicily. This mosaic was created by Byzantine craftsmen for the Normans who were occupying Sicily. It thus represents the intersection of East and West in the Eleventh Century.

CHRISTIAN BELIEVING

CHRISTIAN BELIEVING

ROBERT E. TERWILLIGER

MOREHOUSE-BARLOW CO.
Wilton, Connecticut

Printed in the United States of America

FOR ANNE

Preface

This book should be read fast. It is intended as a stimulus, not a study. Its purpose is to say one thing: Christian believing is an action; something we do because of something the Holy Spirit does in us. It is an involving action which draws us into an experience of God and a great belonging in the body of the Risen Christ.

The titles of chapters have a verbal form—"Knowing the Bible," "Living the Liturgy," "Thinking Theologically," Praying Continually"—to express the ways of active participation in which Christian believing occurs. These ways are not optional; they are the essential experiences which keep creating conviction. A failure in any one of them can cause a "crisis of faith."

My joyful discovery of the tradition of the Eastern Churches reveals itself throughout this book. So many Western Christians seem to be making this discovery simultaneously that it seems to be part of the present purpose of God for us.

Behind this book are several years of my ministry. During this critical period in the church's life, I have been Director of Trinity Institute, bringing it into existence. This theological center for the Episcopal clergy nationally is a place of encounter between bishops, priests, and deacons and the more affirmative makers of theology in both Europe and America. The excitement of this work has been tremendous, both from the stimulation of the theologians who have visited us, and from the hundreds of clergy who have kept responding. I have also been called upon to conduct diocesan clergy conferences and to give series of lectures for lay people throughout the United States. Continuing dialogue with my students of the General Theological Seminary, where I am an adjunct professor, has further contributed to my education.

These experiences convince me that this is a time for affirmation. The church has been suffering from failure of nerve in Christian believing. Faith always involves risk; it is time we took that risk, and said again—I believe!

ROBERT E. TERWILLIGER

Acknowledgments

The author acknowledges the kind permission of the following for use of the copyrighted material indicated:

Longman Group Ltd: *Mysterium Christi, Christological Studies by British and German Theologians,* by G. K. A. Bell and D. A. Deissmann, London, 1930.

Charles Scribner's Sons: *God Was in Christ: An Essay on Incarnation and Atonement,* by D. M. Baillie, New York, 1948.

Harcourt Brace Jovanovich, Inc: *Diary 1928-1957* by Julien Green, selected by Kurt Wolff, tr. Anne Green, New York, 1964.

Kallistos Ware and Penguin Books: *The Orthodox Church,* by Timothy Ware, London and Baltimore, 1963.

The University of Chicago Press: *The Emergence of the Catholic Tradition* by Jaroslav Pelikan, © 1971 The University of Chicago Press, Chicago and London.

Most Biblical quotations herein are from *The New English Bible* © The Delegates of the Oxford University Press and The Syndics of the Cambridge University Press 1961, 1970. Reprinted by permission. Quotations marked RSV are from *The Holy Bible: Revised Standard Version,* copyright © 1952, 1946 by the Division of Christian Education of the National Council of Churches of Christ in the United States of America.

Table of Contents

CHAPTER I

Believing in Jesus Christ

JESUS IS LORD—this was the earliest Christian creed. It was enough; for in those three words is concentrated the whole of Christian faith. Christian believing is believing in the Lordship of Jesus, but it must be the real Jesus, the whole Jesus, the Jesus of the New Testament.

At first sight this may seem like a simple faith, a one-item confession, that stands in refreshing contrast to the creeds, the liturgies, the volumes upon volumes of theological writing that the succeeding centuries have produced. "Jesus is Lord" is an affirmation which the humblest person can make, but, at the same time, it is capable of an infinite expansion of meaning. It has converted barbarians; it has also consumed the genius of Thomas Aquinas and Teilhard de Chardin. It is not that Christian faith can be reduced to a single idea, but that there is in that one person, Jesus, an inexhaustible revelation of the mystery of God and of man; indeed the whole truth of the cosmos.

This is a very different conception of what is involved in faith from the all too popular notion that being a Christian means saying "yes" to a whole list of propositions beginning with the existence of God and ending, I suppose, with heaven. In between come all sorts of items like the inspiration of the Bible, the atonement, the Holy Spirit, the importance of prayer, and monogamous marriage—all unrelated. Christian faith does not develop by accumulation; though, it has to be confessed, that is sometimes the way it has been presented and upheld.

Everything in Christian believing originates in one source, Jesus: in what he said, in how he lived, in what has happened because of him—in what he is. The Christian Faith is the unfolding of the inevitable implications of this man. He is the cause of the affirmations of the creeds of the church; the liturgies of Christendom stem from him; he is the originator of Christian theology and its perpetual theme, and all these expressions of faith are validly Christian only when they are true to him.

This zeroing in on Jesus is shocking; it shocked men in the first century and it shocks them now. In New Testament language this focus on Jesus is a scandal, in Greek, *skandalon,* which means a snare, a cause of stumbling, something to trip over mentally, morally, or spiritually. It interrupts a man who is on his way; it makes him stop, perhaps stop and think; even stop and believe—it staggers him.

People do not believe the Christian faith because it can be reduced to noncontroversial statements; because there is no difference between what Christians believe and what everybody else believes, between their world view and the world view of their own culture. They believe it because there *is* a difference. There is an offense in the Gospel which has always shocked men and ought to shock them. Where such a scandal occurs, we have a signal of the supernatural, of God's action. It is in the hard sayings of Jesus, the paradoxical doctrines of faith, not in the easy, unimpeded movement of thought and experience, that we find—may I say it—the temptation to believe. Then we can feel the excitement which Tertullian expressed in his vivid exaggeration: "I believe because it is absurd."

The scandal of this focus on Jesus is called in theological language "the scandal of particularity." So far as I know, the term was first used by the German biblical scholar Gerhard

Kittel, although the fact is as old as Christianity itself. It means quite simply that at a particular time, in a particular place, among a particular people, and through a particular person, God deliberately participated in human history. There he disclosed himself definitively and acted decisively for the redemption of the world.

When I think of "the scandal of particularity," I always think of the phrase "one grain of sand," for this is the vivid metaphor which Kittel himself used in his rather Germanic phrasing about the event which was Jesus:

Somewhere in the course of centuries something has once occurred. Yes, but that which we name humanity and human history is just a formless mass of innumerable lives which have run their course, and it resembles a huge heap of sand. Can we dare to select *one grain of sand* and claim for it uniqueness and peculiarity? And yet that is precisely what in fact we do.[1]

"One grain of sand"—realize the absurdity of this! One historical person, one event, among billions of persons, and millennia of human happenings. Furthermore, as Kittel points out, when we consider what kind of individual he was, and when and where he lived, why focus on him?

Neither the land where he lived nor the people among whom he dwelt was marked as the centre of mighty empire or of a brilliant civilization. The famous Roman historians regarded Judea as one of the most obscure corners of the Empire, and Galilee as even more obscure. And if a Jew suffered a martyr's death by crucifixion in Jerusalem, well the Romans erected many crosses, and both then and always there have been many martyrs, the majority of whom were in their deaths, humanly speaking, far more noble, far more heroic, than he who dies with the miserable cry upon his lips, *My God, my God, why hast thou forsaken me?*[2]

Yet Christians do focus on this Jesus, because of, not in spite of, this absurdity:

The foolishness of God is wiser than men. . . (I Corinthians 1:25) Here is declared the singularity of the New Testament message; and this is the miracle of which it speaks from the first page to the last. The New Testament tells nothing that is obviously comprehensible. It tells of a "miracle" in the strict and proper sense of the word. *The Word became flesh,* that is to say, what is eternal became historical, accidental, and miserably insignificant, and this poor and trivial contingency contains— God himself.[3]

Why would anyone believe a thing like that: that in this Jesus, in one individual, can be found a world-view and a God-view, in fact the absolute meaning of all that there is? Why would anyone believe that in the particularity of Jesus is the particularity of God; that the One and Only God was acting in Christ? What kind of disturbing figure provokes such a reaction?

Read one of the gospels straight through, preferably the shortest and the earliest, Mark. Let the figure of Jesus emerge before you. For too long we have been losing the figure of Jesus by taking the New Testament in snippets by a lectionary or some scheme of daily readings, but the time has come for "getting it all together." You will also find things he did and said that you have forgotten—perhaps repressed.

Then read Matthew, and then Luke in the same way. These three are the "synoptic gospels," so called from the Greek word meaning "with one eye," for they all look at the same events in the life of Jesus. Realize that these books are not biographies of a man by three solitary individuals. They are the work of the early communities of faith in the Mediterranean world, the gathering up of the sayings and stories of Jesus that had been current in the church's preaching and worship before they were forgotten. There is an excitement about Jesus in the gospels which is one of the most important things in them, for the excitement which Jesus created is a fact about his life. It is best to use one of the new modern versions so that the vividness of this excitement can reach you. These books were not written "for the record"; they were written to put you in touch with Christ.

The Fourth Gospel, St. John, is so different in chronology, vocabulary, and obvious purpose that you will sense it is an interpretation of the meaning of the life of Jesus, a rearranging and retelling of the story to embrace his life in the experience of Christians in the earliest church. For that very reason it is the richest of the four gospels.

When you have read these four short books, you will have covered all of the certain sources for the life of Jesus. The figure who appears in all the gospels is clear. He is a teacher, but his teaching has an unnerving authority about it. He insists on the necessity of justice and—a word we seldom use these days—of righteousness. He also teaches the demand of a love which burns out all sentimentality in a total passion of self-giving—first to God and then to neighbor, particularly the needy and rejected neighbor. This love requires unbelievable acts of forgiveness, even of enemies, which are a condition for being forgiven oneself.

The Jesus of the gospels is apt to say things his followers prefer to forget, such as his requirement of total sexual purity even in imagination, the God-made cohesiveness of marriage, the damnable dangers of the sins of religion, and the possibility of a destiny in hell. He teaches his ethic not as good advice but as the law of God, who will see to it that the whole human race comes to terms with his demands in a final judgment.

Jesus also heals the sick by what appears to be a charismatic gift. All the gospels bear witness to the strange good things that happen when he appears to people in desperate straits of body and of mind.

He also takes action against those who exploit others and who live hypocritically. He makes immediate dangerous enemies among the powerful political and religious classes in his little nation. This forms a bond which cannot be broken between him and all those who suffer to right wrong and have a passion for remaking society into a pattern of just order. But he offends the revolutionary because he rejects violence and teaches non-resistance to evil, because his Kingdom is not of this world.

His Kingdom, the Kingdom of God, is the perpetual burden of his teaching. It is not an idyllic dream, or the program for some kind of politics; it is the coming of the New Era. In him the Reign of God had broken into the world for the first and final time, and he is the bringer of it. Those who imply that there is a paranoid insistence in this theme hear him better than those who perceive nothing in his words but a blissful spiritual teaching. There is no obscuring the fact that in his deeds and in his words there is an emerging consciousness of his own special function in the Reign. He feels acutely that he has a peculiar place in the scheme of God's action and communication with men. It rises to a terrific peak in his words: "Everything is entrusted to me by my Father; . . .and no one knows the Father but the Son and those to whom the Son may choose to reveal him." (Matthew 11:27). The often-quoted words of consolation which follow immediately are no less self-affirming, but they are usually severed from their context; "Come to me, all whose work is hard, whose load is heavy; and I will give you relief. Bend your necks to my yoke, and learn from me, for I am gentle and humble-hearted; and your souls will find relief. For my yoke is good to bear, my load is light" (Matthew 11:28-29).

The climax of the gospels is the story of his last days. Each of the gospels spends a quarter to a third of its attention on the passion and its outcome. Jesus deliberately goes down to Jerusalem where he will predictably endanger his life in order to preach the Reign of God and his part in it.

There may be discussion among scholars about the vocabulary in which Jesus declared his own specialness—Son of Man, Messiah, Son of God—but there can scarcely be any question about the unequivocal meaning of his entry into Jerusalem. He is acting out his claim to be the Deliverer who was expected. The cleansing of the Temple, all of the words of challenge to Jerusalem, are full of his awareness that he had something necessary to do for the human race. Throughout his whole life Jesus is the servant of God by being the servant of man, but Jesus believes his greatest service is to be the giving of his own life for the world. The healer and the helper, the prophet of righteousness, is the man who must fulfill now, not another service but the consummation of his whole life as a servant in this final act.

Jesus makes this absolutely clear at the Last Supper when he reinterprets the ancient ritual acts pertaining to the Passover, reinterprets them in his own name, to signify his own awful God-destined death, through which he must pass to the Kingdom. He himself is now to be the sacrifice. The whole age-old drama of Good against Evil is to reach its denouement in that moment.

This conviction of his unique and terrible destiny makes him stay there praying in the bloody sweat of Gethsemane till they finally take him. Through the travesty of a trial to the final atrocity of the crucifixion, he submits to death, and finally to the darkest disaster of all: "My God, my God, why have you forsaken me?"

Then the Gospel begins. The Gospel begins with the resurrection—not ends, but begins with it. It was the resurrection which made the life and death of Jesus Gospel, Good News. Had his story ended with his cry, "My God, My God, why?" and if this end was decently obscured by burial in a borrowed tomb, then the life of Jesus would have decisively demonstrated what the universe does with men like him. But the story does not stop there. The end is the beginning, an act of God, which authenticates Jesus' driving faith in his own particularity and gives him to the world as its Christ.

There is no way to separate the life and the teaching of Jesus from his claim to Christhood. No original document about Jesus exists which does not contain this claim in one form or another. To separate the claim from the rest of the Gospel would be such an act of expurgation that the very motivation for his end is eliminated. It used to be popular to distinguish between the "religion of Jesus" and "the religion about Jesus," but the religion of Jesus was about Jesus, and it drove him to his death.

There is no Jesus in any record who does not claim to be the Christ; nor if that claim is not authenticated, is he a "man for others," anywhere, anytime; he is a man at best deluded in his essential self-understanding, at worst, a charlatan. But the Gospel declares that the claim is authenticated; that God did something about him to show that it is true. What God did is the reason Christians accept the scandal of particularity.

"Jesus is Lord"—the earliest Christian creed is the proclamation of the Living Christ, the affirmation of the resurrection. First century Christians knew as well as twentieth century Christians that resurrections do not happen. Therefore, when one does, when the impossible has occurred, it has within it the secret of history and the revelation of God. This particular man, this Jesus, is Lord of all!

CHAPTER II

Experiencing the Resurrection

A story appeared on the front page of *The New York Times* of Sunday, January 3, 1971, reporting the discovery of the skeleton of a young man crucified in Jerusalem about the time of Christ. It was an archeological find which reputedly threw light on the Roman method of crucifixion, which was different from the way it is usually represented in Christian crucifixes. The ankle bones had been nailed through. It was said that there was no evidence that the skeleton was that of Jesus since several thousand people were crucified there during that period. But could it have been?

The question has to be faced: Could the body ever be found? Would finding the body destroy Christian faith? Can a modern Christian actually believe in the resurrection—for that matter, in life after death?

Questioning the resurrection was once the province of unbelievers. Ever since the Enlightenment it has been a matter of course that secular rationalists would scoff at the very idea of resurrection. More recently such skepticism and even disbelief has emerged within Christianity itself. It is of more than one sort; for instance, a doubt about the possibility of miracle at all, the suspicion that the resurrection of Jesus is but another myth of a dying and rising savior-god, skepticism about the reliability of New Testament records.

A new kind of attack has come by the device of saying that the resurrection could not possibly be what it plainly means, the restoration of Jesus to life, but that it must mean something else, at least to modern man. The passionate ideology called "demythologization," instigated by the German theologian Rudolph Bultmann, contended that a scientific world view was absolute for twentieth century man. What first century New Testament man stated in mythological form has to be transmuted into thought forms—in Bultmann's case, existentialist—acceptable to modern man. The resurrection thus becomes the apostles' perception that the cross was not a defeat, but a victory. Then came the onslaught of the secularization of the gospel in its various forms, which insisted that the resurrection had to mean something non-religious, indeed, an attitude, not a happening. It turned out to be something like contagious freedom caught from the powerful freedom of Jesus. These tendencies produced appalling reductions of Christian faith which resulted in denying the possibility of any direct divine manifestation in the material world, and leaving the mental and the moral the only domain for faith.

For some decades now it has seemed that questioning the resurrection is one of the credentials for intellectual credibility. I remember once being regaled with a story about a brilliant academic who preached a series of sermons on the life of Christ. The preacher, it was said, was "so learned that he left him hanging on the cross."

Not all learning now leaves Christ "hanging on the cross." A powerful theological movement in recent years has been the Theology of Hope. It is the work of a brilliant circle of young German theologians, led by Wolfhardt Pannenberg and Jürgen Moltmann. It centers on a reaffirmation of the resurrection in demanding volumes of the most careful scholarly research and theological method. Such books as Pannenberg's *Jesus: God and Man* and Moltmann's *The Theology of Hope* provide a new apologetic for the resurrection and a fresh insight into its meaning. Christians are thinking again about the resurrection.

The starting point has to be the witness of the earliest Christians. "Jesus is Lord" meant Jesus has been raised from the dead and is known to us as the Living Christ. In the New Testament the Gospel *is* the resurrection. This is the greatest scandal of the Christian faith, but it is the belief which causes conversion, and on which the early Christians dare to take their stand. The resurrection gives them their identity as Christians. Paul writes concretely and vividly to the obstreperous church in Corinth reminding them what their commitment was:

And now, my brothers, I must remind you of the gospel that I preached to you; the gospel which you received, on which you have taken your stand, and which is now bringing you salvation. Do you still hold fast the Gospel as I preached it to you? If not, your conversion was in vain.

First and foremost, I handed on to you the facts which had been imparted to me: that Christ died for our sins, in accordance with the scriptures; that he was buried; that he was raised to life on the third day, according to the scriptures; and that he appeared to Cephas, and afterwards to the Twelve. Then he appeared to over five hundred of our brothers at once, most of whom are still alive, though some have died. Then he appeared to James, and afterwards to all the apostles.

In the end he appeared even to me. It was like an abnormal birth; I had persecuted the church of God and am therefore inferior to all other apostles—indeed not fit to be called an apostle. However, by God's grace I am what I am, nor has his grace been given to me in vain; on the contrary, in my labours I have outdone them all—not I, indeed, but the grace of God working with me. But what matter, I or they? This is what we all proclaim, and this is what you believed. (I Corinthians 15:1-11)

It should be remembered that these witnesses he mentioned were still around, so Paul could not afford a flight of imagination. But to be a Christian was not simply to have seen something—the Risen Lord—or have accepted the fact that someone else had seen something. The believer had been offered an experience of the Christ even if he never laid eyes on him. The Scottish theologian, D.M. Baillie, wrote movingly about this discovery of the earliest believers, who found that

... this experience, which depended entirely on Jesus, need not be confined to those who had known Jesus in the flesh. It could come to anybody anywhere through the story of Jesus and their witness to its meaning. They went hither and thither and told the story; and the thing kept happening. It was a new experience of God, and it lifted people out of themselves, and above the moral struggle, into a spontaneous goodness which claimed no credit for itself but gave all the glory to God. It could not have come if Jesus had not lived. It all depended on Him. And yet it was different from the experience of knowing Jesus in the flesh—not less, but greater, deeper, more universal, more transforming. [4]

If this is the true experience of the resurrection, do modern Western Christians even know what the resurrection is? The early Christian bore witness to a reality that we have as barely glimpsed when we believed it as when we denied it. Historically, our feeble sense of the power and joy of the resurrection may stem from the almost exclusive focus on the passion and the crucifixion in late medieval piety in Western Europe. This resulted in the upside-down pattern of a great emphasis on Lent and Holy Week in popular devotion, but the virtual loss of the Great Fifty Days of Eastertide. We prepare for forty days for a festival we do not celebrate!

To repossess the reality of the resurrection, to experience its actuality, we must learn again what it is. This requires recovering three essential dimensions of its meaning.

The resurrection of Christ is the onset of the New Creation. Jesus risen is the New Man—in the language of Paul, the Second Adam: "As in Adam all men die, so in Christ all will be brought to life" (I Corinthians 15:22). "If any one is in Christ, he is a new creation; the old has passed away, behold, the new has come" (II Corinthians 5:17, RSV). The resurrection brought newness into the divine-human relation; in Baillie's words, "It was a new experience of God." St. John sees the fulfillment of this resurrection-newness in his vision in the Apocalypse: "Then I saw a new heaven and a new earth" (Revelation 21:1).

The newness of the resurrection comes from the fulfillment of Jesus' own self-understanding, of his claim to be the Saving Person, the Bringer of redemption. The resurrection is the revelation of the truth of that claim. It is therefore a *unique* event because it authenticates his uniqueness.

It is difficult to think "unique." "Unique" means something in and of itself, something that never was before, something that never happened after. When we say that the resurrection is a unique event, unique with Christ's own uniqueness, unique with God's own singling out of the cross and reversing it, we are making an astounding statement about history.

Christians do not believe in the resurrection of Jesus because resurrections happen all the time, or even occasionally. They do not regard this event as, for instance, a spiritualist would: a very special instance of the common manifestation of a human who has passed over to "the other side." Christians believe that there never was another event like this because there never was another Christ.

The uniqueness of the resurrection runs counter to the way we have come to understand history. It is as common as the air we breathe to assume that an educated man knows what can and what cannot happen in history. This calm assumption may be shattered periodically by some catastrophic surprise for good or evil which we call "a history-making event." In the ultimate sense the resurrection is *the history-making event,* showing what is now possible through Christ. Something like this is implied even in the calendar, which dates years before and after Christ.

If the resurrection is unique in the exact sense, then it is impossible to say whether it could or could not happen, because it is precisely not just one other event in the ordinary stream of history which is subject to prediction and control. There is no "scientific" approach to the question, because science depends on the normal course of happenings to establish its probabilities. It has to be said that the concept of science as the record of exact "laws" is more eighteenth than twentieth century, and a modern scientist who went into his laboratory assured of what he could and could not find would discover nothing.

The nature of the uniqueness of the resurrection is further illuminated by realizing the meaning of the word "Resurrection" is an Old Testament term. It has to do with awakening, with the final awakening from death on the Last Day. It is, therefore, a word oriented—quite literally oriented, facing east, facing the rising sun—toward what the day is to bring. We do not just awake, we *awake to* something. Everyone recalls memorable instances of such *awakening to,* some dreadful, some glorious: "This is the day that. . . ." In scriptural language, the resurrection is the day that the Lord made, and it faces the future.

The Theologians of Hope have coined a startling phrase for this orientation: "the Future of Jesus Christ." Jesus has a future—not only a past, but a future! It is not all over; Jesus awakens to a destiny for himself which is the destiny of history. God will consummate the unique purpose of his life. The resurrection reveals the consequence: "he must reign" (I Corinthians 15:25).

Christ which comes toward us in history and goes beyond us to the End of it All. The Christian view can, then, never be nostalgia, a backward look, but a forward look from the empty tomb. The resurrection is the concrete ground of Christian hope.

The resurrection of Christ is the triumph of the cross. Easter faith is not the happy ending of the story of the passion, just a glimpse of glory which reassures us that God set Calvary straight. Christ did not escape from pain and death; he overcame them. He did not get away from it all; he conquered it all. The crucifixion and the resurrection are one; Good Friday and Easter are one.

The ancient and greatest hymns of the cross are triumphant; in fact, they have a military ring about them:

> The royal banners forward go,
> The cross shines forth in mystic glow
> Where he, as man, who gave man breath,
> Now bows beneath the yoke of death. [5]

> Sing, my tongue, the glorious battle,
>   Sing the winning of the fray;
> Now above the cross, the trophy,
>   Sound the high triumphal lay:
> Tell how Christ, the world's Redeemer,
>   As a victim won the day. [6]

The hymns of Easter also incorporate the suffering and death of the cross as the ground of their praise, as in the ode of the cosmic warfare of Christ sung in the Easter Sequence:

Death and life have contended
In that combat stupendous:
The Prince of Life, who died,
    reigns immortal. [7]

And again in the powerful seventeenth century words:

The strife is o'er, the battle done,
The victory of life is won;
The song of triumph has begun.
            Alleluia!
Lord! by the stripes which wounded thee,
From death's dread string thy servants free,
That they may live and sing to thee.
            Alleluia! [8]

The same motif can be seen in the first crucifixes, before Christians became obsessed with picturing the writhing, anguished Christ. The greatest Christian iconography of the cross shows this unity. The best crucifix never evokes pity. It is always in some way a triumph crucifix. In the bearing of the figure, or in symbolic form, it signifies both the reality of the evil suffered and the death, and also the victory over it.

Gustaf Aulén, the Swedish bishop-theologian, revived an awareness of this theme in the modern church by his great book, *Christus Victor.* This work showed that the original, "classic" atonement motif was Christ's conquest of the powers of evil which destroy us, by taking their full force upon himself and annihilating their strength. The resurrection thus shows God's way of dealing with the problem of evil.

Christian faith does not give a theoretical solution, but a practical one—God did something about evil in Christ. Easter thus means that all the suffering, physical and mental, which Christ went through, the real and total death which destroyed him, he underwent undeservedly to give his conquest to all mankind. The resurrection is not his personal triumph, but God's gift of the Living Lord in communion with whom we can share in his victory. This is all *pro nobis*, for us. This faith can obviously never be reduced to completely rational statements. It belongs to the great and true mythological patterns which say more in poetry than in propositions.

But more mysteriously still, the *Christus Victor* motif speaks to man's condition of bondage to evil which separates him from God. By our consent to sin we lose our freedom. It always seems that we assert our freedom by disobedience, but in fact we forfeit it. The old language about this speaks of bondage to the devil, and before we reject the idea as absurd, let us realize that this motif has a sudden pertinence, as the "Jesus freak" has found. The predicament of the addict reveals in a terrible way the predicament of us all when we lose our freedom by consent to evil. The "Jesus freak" has found that the experience of the saving Christ even breaks the bonds of drugs, and gives him a new life in God. Christ who has entered the domain of darkness and put himself in the place of sinners destroys the chains of their imprisonment and sets them free. This is the original theme of Christ as Redeemer—freeing men from their slavery, to unite them to the Father. "God was in Christ reconciling the world to himself" (II Corinthians 5:19, RSV).

The icon of the resurrection in the Eastern Church is not of Jesus rising from the tomb—which no one witnessed—or of his being seen in the garden. It is the resurrection of the second day, not the third: it is the Christ who has descended into the underworld, grasping Adam by the hand and pulling Adam up.

The resurrection of Christ transforms his body. Jesus was all there in his resurrection. This was no partial Jesus, no purely spiritual man, no ghostly, disembodied spirit; nor was it simply visions. All of these approaches might show that Jesus had in some sense survived death, but not that he had totally conquered it. Furthermore, it is the body of Christ which is the link between the cross and the resurrection. The stories rejoice to say that the disciples identified Jesus by the wound-prints.

When Jesus died, he was really dead. He was as dead as the dog run over in the street. The veritable Christian faith has no place for the notion that his death was only apparent: that he, and perhaps we, only seem to die. The Christian doctrine is resurrection, not immortality. Immortality means that it is a characteristic of man to live forever. It is really a notion from non-Christian sources. The death was real, and in a classic Christian phrase, the resurrection is the "death of death." And death happens to bodies; it is a constant process in all organisms, so that it belongs to the very stuff of life. What Christians believe is that God did something about the death of Jesus in his own decisive act of raising him again in the body.

It seems very strange to me that in this age when we are so full of body awareness, when we have delightfully discovered the goodness of the body, Christians should recoil from the idea of bodily resurrection. Is the physical still revolting? What other kinds of persons are there than embodied persons? Surely we are thoroughly saturated with the awareness of psycho-somatic unity, the body and the psyche indissolubly united. Underlying the shrinking from the resurrection of the body, it appears to me, is a squeamishness about the flesh, an incipient Gnosticism, which was the prime heresy of the early church.

What is at stake in the resurrection of the body is the humanity of Christ. He is unique in a complete newness, and yet he is one of us. He had a mind, which requires a brain; he touched and healed, which required hands; he had all of our physical animal nature. His physicality is the link between him and the whole material universe. And in the resurrection he is all together. The tomb was empty.

Part of our problem about the resurrection of the body is that we assume that "body" is a simple idea. Critics of the doctrine sometimes refer to it as "the resuscitation of a corpse" and ask contemptuously if there had been a photograph taken, would there have been anything on the film.

We cannot know altogether what we are talking about when we say resurrection of the "body." It has to mean in some way the physicality of Jesus. God did not reject the crucified body of Christ. But when we try to describe body we face the same problem we do with human bodies everywhere. Body is a process, it is a means of expression of mind and spirit, it is a means of communication between persons. It comes and goes even in the course of earthly life. It changes form and cellular content periodically. And yet it is the material and the energy with which we think, and act, and love. Without it we are not.

But what of resurrected body? The stories of the events reveal a difference: Jesus has not returned to resume his old life; he is different. He is discernibly different; he has a new freedom to appear and to disappear, to come and to go when doors were locked. Yet he is the same—"Look at my hands and feet. It is I myself" (Luke 24:39).

The body had been in some way taken up and transformed, transmuted. Paul gives a radical metaphor for all this in his great resurrection discourse in the fifteenth chapter of First Corinthians where he speaks of mortal bodies and resurrection bodies as the seed and the flower with death as the planting.

The point is the purpose: the body of Christ is to be glorified and to be given. It is raised into the state in which it is to be united to God, as is indicated by the final resurrection appearance which we call the Ascension. It is also to be given, for the embodied life of Christ is the new creation God starts in Jesus for mankind and the whole of the cosmos. The body of Christ is to be communicated for the restoration of the world, filling all things. It seems inevitable, at least in our era, to speak of it in terms of a perfect, pure, created energy which is capable of being the instrument whereby God recreates the world, eventually penetrating all that there is, en-Christing it.

So far as the photographer is concerned, how does it photograph? It might destroy the film, except that God does not use Christ to destroy creation. At least it is *more than, not less than* a human form as we know it. The language of transfiguration may be the best way to express all of this. The risen body is Christ's body radiating the transforming power and glory of his life to us.

Is there any objective evidence for the resurrection happening? The records in the New Testament of the event are not consistent. Consistent records would, of course, be disastrous proof of tampering with reports. Human beings cannot agree unanimously on an automobile accident, to say nothing of the resurrection of the dead. Belief in the resurrection does not require a "for the Bible tells me so" fundamentalism. An educated Christian should study the New Testament evidence, reading more than devotional books. There is an impressive and demanding literature which requires a kind of study which ought not to be shunned by those who really want to give the reason for the faith that is in them.

The greatest objective evidence for the resurrection is the Christian Church, which was the consequence of the resurrection. The dramatic and drastic change which came over the apostles requires an explanation. It was too lasting and too creative to have been the result of self-deception or madness and hallucinations. The earliest church sprang up so quickly, with such motivation and energy, with such phenomenal geographical spread, that it simply had to be powered by some impulse of stupendous impact. Something happened!

This church has persisted through history, taking hold in every kind of race and culture, surviving all kinds of attempts to exterminate it, even thriving on them. It has also kept reproducing in saints and even in sinners a kind of character which shows the lineaments of the life of Christ; and this church has shown a power of surviving even evil within its own membership, which implies a life indwelling its members which is not just their own.

The Christian life itself is an experience of death and resurrection. This has been the testimony of every generation of the church. These things keep happening within it: conversions of life, forgiveness of sin, healings of mind and of body, transformations of whole peoples, the creation of social change by the church's bringing new achievements of justice, sudden eruptions of unspeakable beauty in centuries of unselfconscious art. The myriad forms of resurrection in the millennia of the church are governed by something more powerful than a common psychic pattern; they are governed by an event, something that really happened in the center of things, and the evidence is that it can happen to *you.*

The only clinching evidence of the resurrection is quite simply knowing the Risen Lord. This experience can sometimes come in an intense sense of his living presence, but it does not have to be mystical at all. In a real sense the rest of this book is about the resurrection and knowing it in the many relationships which constitute Christian believing, because the whole of Christian faith is being involved with the Living Christ.

In these days when one experience is worth a million words, all that I have been trying to say in this chapter can be grasped by being present at the liturgy of an Eastern church. The Orthodox have preserved a sense of the presence of the Risen Lord more powerfully than the churches of the West. In our need to recover the original New Testament faith in the resurrection we can do nothing better than to stay a while with them as they worship.

A visit to an Eastern Orthodox church is like entering another world to a Western Christian. A sense of luminous mystery pervades the whole place. The glow of many candles reflects on the burnished surfaces, the strange unearthly figures range row upon row on the iconostasis, like the very presence of the saints in heaven. The penetrating odor of incense fills the holy space.

Above it all, and looking through it all, there is the icon of the Living Christ. In an ancient church this was a figure of tremendous majesty and power, representing Christ the Logos, the Word, the Pantocrator, who fills all things. This

Christ looks directly at you, searching you out wherever you are, and finding you with a gaze of yearning and triumphant peace. (Note: see the cover picture.)

As the worship proceeds, interminably to a Westerner, he comes into a new time sense, or better, into a new sense of eternity. The voice of the choirs, which enthrall even the unbeliever, joined often by the spontaneous singing of the congregation, makes the whole church seem to throb with a divine life. But in the midst of all this vibrant glory there is a marvelous at-homeness with the holy—the bishop taking his crown-mitre and combing his hair, the old women walking through the congregation with baskets full of blessed bread, the man in a business suit reverently venerating the icon, the teen-age server in brocaded vestments and sneakers—for all are at home with the Lord who comes to them in bread and wine.

No Christian communion has suffered more persecution than the Eastern Church, and none has shown more power of survival. No small part of its secret lies in this constant sense of the presence of Christ. It persisted when the cathedrals and churches in Russia were closed, destroyed, or converted to secular use. When millions of that church went into exile in Western Europe and America, in the homes, garages and barns where they had to worship, these Orthodox rediscovered the true glory of the perpetual liturgy of the Risen Lord.

The real presence of the resurrection is the incessant witness of the Orthodox, and many of us gratefully acknowledge our debt to them for our discovery of its reality. They show us what the New Testament testifies, that the resurrection is an actuality; that it is not merely an event in the past but an experience we can enter into. The intense awareness of this truth in the Eastern Church perpetuates the faith of the New Testament.

The Christian who has entered into this mystery of the resurrection himself will not worry that the skeleton found by an archeologist in Jerusalem is the skeleton of Jesus of Nazareth.

CHAPTER III

Receiving the Holy Spirit

The Holy Spirit has suddenly excited the imagination of Christians. The Charismatic, or Pentecostal, Movement has come into the church with unexpected power, making utterly necessary a new consideration of this almost forgotten aspect of the Christian experience of God. Not only in marginal Christian groups, but in the most conventional churches, people are speaking in tongues, testifying to powerful and even miraculous outpourings of spiritual gifts, and expressing a new joy and peace in believing. It is strange to remember those recent days when the doctrine of the Holy Spirit was neglected, if not disparaged, as part of the rejection of the Trinity of God.

The resurgence has a context. It is a manifestation of the present dramatic quest for the experience of the transcendent. It comes as a radical contradiction of the antireligious tendency which previously characterized secular society and even the church. Such an occurrence is a sign which must be read carefully, because it says something important about human nature and Christian nature which can be ignored only with peril.

The upsurge of religious interest has demonstrated that technological society cannot provide the deep spiritual satisfactions which people must have to survive in our era. Science and materialism are not enough. The growing fascination for Eastern religions, the popularity of astrology, the curiosity about possible preternatural and satanic manifestations, and, most apparent of all, the drug culture, with its quest for another dimension, or escape from it all—these demonstrate that "modern man" has to go beyond himself in order to exist.

The quest for transcendence is not primarily intellectual, as it has been so often before; it is emotional. This may be the result of the terrible pace of change and its demand for the reassurance of instant experience. Our attention span is decreasing. The new media, with their appeal to the visual and the auditory, have created a new psychology more focused on feeling and sensation. We have become a people who have difficulty not only reading but thinking; yet we can feel more quickly, if not more deeply, than we have for centuries.

The Charismatic Movement and its counterpart, "the Jesus Movement," have appeared as a repossession of the elements of feeling in religion that conventional Christians had forgotten, if not rejected. There has been a starvation of emotion in the church. Now that is disappearing in what sometimes seems like a binge of religious excitement. These things have happened before in Christian history, and they have always had two characteristics: first, they represent a necessary correction of direction in the Church's life; and second, they have a relatively short duration. They are a signal for Christians to become quickly aware that something is lacking, and to think more profoundly about the neglected aspects of belief and life.

The greatest expression of the Holy Spirit in the church in our time, however, may mot be in movements of religious enthusiasm but in the miracle of the new ecumenism. We have by now become so used to the wonderful openness and desire for unity which our era has enjoyed that we hardly remember the days of separation, barely a decade ago, before it all began. Pope John, the Vatican Council, the sudden fruition of the long years of Protestant-Orthodox-Anglican ecumenism—all of this must not be taken for granted. Christians are in the grip of something they did not plan, contrive, expect, or too often even want. We have not so much come together as been knocked together. This is certainly of the Holy Spirit.

"No one can say 'Jesus is Lord!' except under the influence of the Holy Spirit" (I Corinthians 12:3). Faith is not a personal achievement but a gift, a gift of the Spirit. All true Christian believing is a receiving of the Spirit. It is not just an intellectual matter; it is being possessed. A Christian believer is a person to whom something divine has begun to happen, small though that beginning may be.

It may seem that long struggles in becoming convinced of the truth of the Gospel are an intellectual affair and even a personal effort; but in retrospect the Christian does not take credit but gives thanks. Something besides his own ego has been at work within his mind and heart to produce the result. He can never sort out the separate movements of his own will and the Spirit's, but he knows that the joy of believing has come to him, not been achieved by him. It is rather like the experience of falling in love. If I may be forgiven for a slightly flippant illustration—falling in love has been defined as "a lover pursuing his beloved until she gets him." Believing is a man pursuing God, until He gets him. This is the paradox of faith.

Faith in the Jesus of the New Testament involves faith in the Holy Spirit. It is impossible to have the real Jesus without the Holy Spirit, for in the gospels the Spirit is the cause of the life of Christ. Jesus is born by the power of the Spirit; his very earthly existence is the Spirit's work. Jesus' ministry begins with the Spirit descending upon him in his baptism. The early Fathers of the church saw in this event his "ordination." It designates and declares to him his own particularity as the Christ, the Son of the Father.

Then the Spirit drives him into the wilderness to be tempted of the devil. In this dreadful moment of testing, Jesus works through his "crisis of identity" and finds out what his baptism means. This is also the Spirit's work. The Spirit is not always "nice," the sweet bird-like being so often sung about in sentimental hymns. One of the works of the Spirit is terrible testing. The Spirit does not always console. He sometimes disturbs, as he disturbed Jesus, to the very foundation of his being, in an encounter with evil.

The ministry of Jesus is by the power of the Spirit. He announces this in the synagogue at Nazareth, reading the words of the prophet: " 'The spirit of the Lord is upon me because he has anointed me; he has sent me to announce good news to the poor, to proclaim release for prisoners and recovery of sight for the blind; to let the broken victims go free, to proclaim the year of the Lord's favour' " (Luke 4:18-19). His ministry is in continuing conflict with evil, the Other Spirit. Jesus casts our devils by the Holy Spirit. He uttered the most terrible words about those who could not see the Spirit in his deeds. He said that if they claimed his works to be the works of Beelzebub, the Prince of Devils, then they had sinned beyond forgiveness. This text, which has disturbed so many people and even led to mad anxieties about "the unforgivable sin," has this simple meaning: men who had made themselves so unaware of God that they thought the Spirit's acts were the acts of demons were beyond repentance, beyond returning to the God to whom they had blinded themselves.

The passion of Jesus is the final working out of the awful vocation he accepted in the desert. It comes as a consequence of what he had been teaching in the tradition of the prophets of the Old Testament, who spoke by the Spirit. Even as Jerusalem stoned them, so now it destroyed him.

Jesus is raised by the Spirit, and in this decisive act of the Spirit, Christians find their life: "If the Spirit of him who raised Jesus from the dead dwells within you, then the God who raised Christ Jesus from the dead will also give new life to your mortal bodies through his indwelling Spirit" (Romans 8:11).

The life of Christ is Spirit-shaped. A medal created in the Taizé Community of French Protestant monks beautifully symbolizes this truth. It is a circle of brass with the center cut out in the form of a dove-shaped cross (see the back cover of this book). It is worn by those touched by this community as a sign of mission. The dove-shaped cross is a true symbol because the lives of Christians are Spirit-shaped like their Lord's. The New Testament testifies to this.

The Acts of the Apostles tells the story of the earliest church as a story of the Holy Spirit. The original Christian community, gathered and waiting after the Ascension, experiences the supernatural storm of Pentecost. Something happened which was in the nature of a divine possession. It is spoken of in terms of wind and fire, and a gift of tongues. Yet the most important thing about Pentecost was not the strange phenomena, but the radical transformations of those simple, inadequate, weak people into powerful persuaders for the rest of their lives. The text of the Acts is an exciting report, perhaps fanciful in places, of the astounding and unfanciful fact of the missionary spread of the Church throughout the Mediterranean. A new life and joy in Christ sprang up in the ravaged old classical world, bringing a springtime of vitality and faith.

It is a great mistake to take the Acts of the Apostles as the prime and only source for the New Testament experience of the Spirit. The epistles of Paul are of more substantial and permanent value, for they show the meaning of the Holy Spirit.

The unity between Jesus and the Holy Spirit is signified in the writings of Paul by the apparent interchangeable use of the terms "the Spirit of Christ" and "the Holy Spirit." The distinction between Jesus and the Spirit was not formally made in the first emergence of the Spirit-experience. This distinction was left for post-New Testament centuries to articulate. The unity between Jesus and the Spirit shows this essential fact: the living presence and power of Christ cannot be separated from the Spirit, but are the very work of the Spirit. Whoever knows the Living Lord and finds faith in him is experiencing a manifestation of the Spirit.

Paul makes plain that the consequence of the Spirit's action is to change human nature and reproduce the life of Christ in Christians. He wrote to the Galatians about the way the Spirit can be discerned. The Church in Galatia was threatened with destruction by immorality and conflict. This evil condition he describes explicitly: "fornication, impurity, and indecency; idolatry and sorcery; quarrels, a contentious temper, envy, fits of rage, selfish ambitions, dissensions, party intrigues, and jealousies; drinking bouts, orgies, and the like" (Galatians 5:20). The fruits of the Holy Spirit are the exact opposite: "love, joy, peace, patience, kindness, goodness, fidelity, gentleness, and self-control. . . If the Spirit is the source of our life, let the Spirit also direct our course" (Galatians 5:22,25).

Paul is the giver of the apostolic word in the matter of glossolalia. He himself spoke in tongues. Speaking in tongues, then, now, and whenever it has sporadically occurred in Christian history, can be a sign of the Holy Spirit's working. It is a kind of being taken over, of being filled with the joy of intense communion with God. In the course of the experience the believer utters sounds which, though incoherent to a listener, express to him the ineffable fullness of his joy. Often this happens in groups who can go into an unusual synchronization of sound in a togetherness of prayer in the Spirit. The evidence for its being an actual linguistic miracle is unsubstantial. The account of Pentecost in the Acts of the Apostles is probably a reworking of the story in a dramatic way in the light of the known result of Pentecost. The consequence of the gift of the Spirit was, indeed, that "Parthians, Medes, Elamites; inhabitants of Mesopotamia, of Judaea and Cappadocia, of Pontus and Asia, of Phrygia and Pamphylia, of Egypt" and all the other places mentioned in the narrative (Acts 2:10,11). did hear the Word of God.

Glossolalia is a psychological phenomenon which is not confined to Christianity. It should be remembered that there is no evidence whatsoever that Jesus spoke in tongues. Therefore there is no *essential* relation between the Spirit and glossolalia since the baptism of the Spirit which Jesus received was total. Most of the centuries of Christianity have not been periods when this gift was apparent, yet in other ways the Spirit moved with terrific power. Speaking in tongues seems to have a special function of strengthening and reassuring in situations of particular stress or anxiety. It appeared during the traumatic days of the early church. In our own time it seems to have occurred first among the underprivileged and dispossessed in America. Now during a time of breakdown in society, "future shock," and spiritual impoverishment in the church the phenomenon has reappeared. Something like this may have had to happen to make Christians repossess their sense of the supernatural realities of their faith.

The epistles of Paul show that the gift can become divisive (I Corinthians 12). Those who possessed it could become elitist, separating themselves from others. Glossolalia was dangerous when the speakers in tongues thought that they alone had received the Spirit.

Paul makes it clear that speaking in tongues cannot be considered an automatic guarantee of the gift of the Spirit. The only way to discern what spirit was at work in glossalalia or any other phenomenon was to see the result. If it produced love, it was the Holy Spirit. The much-quoted Thirteenth Chapter of First Corinthians—"though I speak with the tongues of men and of angels"—is about speaking with tongues and the gift of the Spirit. It is part of Paul's long directive to that church, which was experiencing schism because of the abuse of this gift.

Receiving the Holy Spirit is never a private and personal affair. In the New Testament it is understood that the Spirit is given in and through the body of Christ. It comes normally by initiation into the church in baptism and laying on of hands. All of this was not at first systematically formulated and defined, but the basic relation between Christian initiation and the Holy Spirit is plain. The Spirit creates the believer's membership in the Christian community by baptism into Christ. This is always the covenanted reception of the Spirit.

One of the good results of the current wave of Pentecostalism has been its better understanding of baptism and the Spirit, of the church in relationship to Spirit, than in the previous similar movement coming out of Protestantism. The present phase has emerged in the Roman Catholic tradition. This environment has permeated it with a more profound understanding of the corporate and sacramental nature of Christian faith. This has given its adherents the awareness that experiencing special gifts of the Spirit is an unfolding in them of the baptismal mystery

The primitive church understood receiving the Spirit as a

gift of truth. When the early Christian was baptized, he was given a candle—a light. Baptism was illumination. The Fourth Gospel discloses this profound perception of the Spirit in the first century. In this gospel Jesus in his farewell discourse tells his disciples about the coming of the Spirit. He shows them that the function of the Spirit is to lead Christians into all truth. He will take the life of Christ and disclose its meaning to them. It is the Spirit which gives the church its understanding of God, including the truth about the Spirit himself.

The New Testament doctrine about the Spirit thus leads beyond the New Testament into the continuing life of the church. The doctrine of the Spirit is developed by the inspiration of the Spirit in history. This is one reason why the fundamentalist with his "Bible only" approach can never fully comprehend the Holy Spirit.

Since the Spirit is the Spirit of truth, the Christian believer has a concern for all truth, not merely religious truth. He is not afraid something true will be discovered which will destroy his faith, for all truth is of the Holy Spirit. He knows that in seeking truth in science, in philosophy, in the movements of history, in other religions, he is being led by the Spirit to see the works of the Spirit.

The development of Christian doctrine, particularly the emergence through conflict of the great consensus which the creeds of the church voice, is the work of the Spirit, and that work is never done. Every generation receives some new illumination, which it gives to the future of faith. The continuity of Christian belief gives evidence of the Spirit's working. It requires some such radical reality as the Holy Spirit to account for the strange persistence of the affirmation of the "scandals" of Christianity. For such an idea as the resurrection of Jesus to be kept alive for twenty centuries implies a supernatural cause.

One of the problems which the new Pentecostalism can unintentionally create is to focus our attention so exclusively on certain special religious experiences that we forget the great and mighty movement of the Holy Spirit through the centuries, which is the greatest evidence.

The Descent of the Dove is the title of a fascinating and exciting book by the lay theologian Charles Williams. It has as its sub-title *A History of the Holy Spirit in the Church.* The genius of this book is the way it reads the long life of the Christian community through all its vicissitudes and sin as the story of response to the Spirit's urging. What emerges is the wonderful awareness that the Holy Spirit has been powerfully present in the church in every age, but even more deeply, that he is moving us into the very life of God, to participate in the very Trinity of God. In receiving the Holy Spirit, Christians are involved with more than an idea or a spiritual sensation: they are drawn into the glorious reality of which the apostle wrote:

For all who are moved by the Spirit of God are sons of God. The Spirit you have received is not a spirit of slavery leading you back into a life of fear, but a Spirit that makes you sons, enabling us to cry "Abba! Father!" In that cry the Spirit of God joins with our spirit in testifying that we are God's children; and if children, then heirs. We are God's heirs and Christ's fellow-heirs, if we share his sufferings now in order to share his splendour hereafter. (Romans 8:14-17)

CHAPTER IV

Belonging in the Church

Edwyn Hoskyns once observed that the questions, "What do you think of Christ?" and "What do you think of the church?" are not two questions but the same question asked in two different ways. [9] In this arresting fashion he asserted the inevitable unity of Christ and his church. It is impossible to have the real Jesus without his church; one is known through the other. Yet this very fact is constantly being controverted.

Right now there are thousands of young people who claim a great joy in the experience of the living presence of Jesus. They will say that they center their religion on "a personal relation to Christ." Yet very often they reject the church, which they find dead to such vital spiritual experience and vastly different from the Jesus who means so much to them. In fact, "the Jesus Movement" in some of its manifestations seems to be anti-church. It distrusts the church as it now exists as a "structure" which must be changed if not eliminated.

The criticism of the church in the name of Jesus has happened before; indeed, it is one of the recurrent projects of the church itself. A basic principle of its life is that the church ought always to be reformed. This can be rightly done only by asking the question of every aspect of its existence: "What has this to do with Jesus of Nazareth?"

Christ against the church can be a plausible and persuasive theme. It can also become in a curious way a denying of the real Christ, for the Jesus of the gospels causes the church.

Did Jesus found the church? At first it may seem hard to get an answer from his mouth. The passage about Peter and the rock is not persuasive because the meaning is ambiguous. Even its authenticity has been questioned, since it is the only place where the actual word "church" is used in the reported vocabulary of Jesus. In addition, we can be hampered in answering the question by the way we are inclined to think of the church as an organization.

The church is not an organization, but an organism. Sometimes this organism exists in an organization, sometimes it is the most simple of social institutions. "When two or three are gathered together," the church is just as much the church as when there is a Vatican or a computerized, structured bureaucracy with national headquarters. The persecuted church of the first three centuries was as much the church as the grand all-embracing institution of medieval Christendom. The question of Jesus' founding the church is not whether he instituted an organization but whether he made inevitable a shaped corporate life for his followers.

Jesus was a Jew. His scripture was the Old Testament. He believed he had to fulfill the law and the prophets. The Hebrew religion was utterly corporate; it was a faith for a people about that people. Israel was a nation which was at once a family and a church. Nothing could be more incredible to a Jew than solitary religion. This was the tradition Jesus believed he was sent to bring to fruition.

When Jesus chose his apostles he made clear that his vision of the future and the heavenly Kingdom was of a new Israel. He chose *twelve* apostles. The Twelve, as the number implies, represented the twelve tribes of Israel. He commissions them to act in his name, and even prophesies that in the Kingdom they will have thrones "judging the twelve tribes of Israel" (Matthew 19:28, RSV). This signifies a new people of God.

The whole teaching of Jesus focuses on the Kingdom of God, the Reign which he brings and which is to fill all the earth. Clearly such a concept is the ultimate in corporateness. This cannot be turned into a purely "spiritual" idea without doing violence to its clear meaning. The teaching about the Kingdom of God is an eschatological concept: that is, it pertains to the *eschaton,* the final End of history. Perhaps Jesus thought it would come soon. We cannot be sure of the time schedule of Jesus' expectation, but whenever the Kingdom should come, it would be a gathering, bringing together humanity from the East and the West. Jesus and his disciples in their mission were the avant-garde of the coming Kingdom.

In the upper room all of this comes into focus when Jesus institutes the common meal of his body and blood which his disciples are to share in the future for the bringing back of him. It is to be the earthly presence of the heavenly banquet of the Kingdom. Here, if nowhere else, it is revealed that Jesus without the church is an incredible idea.

If the church is not formally founded by the teaching and example of Jesus, it is made inevitable. The actual founding, or better, re-founding of the church comes suddenly.

Jesus creates the church by his resurrection. The shock of the appearance of the Risen Lord summons the new People of God. This is indicated in the very etymology of the word for church, *ekklesia,* which signifies an assembly gathered by a herald. The trumpet call which summoned the church was the news of God's raising Jesus from the dead. The resurrection gathers the disciples again. The stories tell again and again of the way the Lord met them *together* and directed them for their future *together.*

On the cross, the People of God was reduced to one; the Old Testament hope that the remnant should be saved was fulfilled, for the remnant was now present in Jesus alone. The church of the Old Covenant passed into the church of the New Covenant in him.

Then the resurrection gave Jesus to the believers, not just as a memory or an idea, but as a Presence. They were united to him in such a total unity that they found he lived in them. This had an inevitable consequence: no one can be "in Christ" without being united with all others who are also in him. The church is thus the result of Christ; indeed, the church in the New Testament is understood to be a continuation of the life of Christ—his body. This never meant that the church was or ever can be the company of the perfect. The church is a redeeming community with the life of the Redeemer at its center continually recreating and cleansing it. That is why baptism with water is the Christian sacramental initiation.

The church is the community of the perpetual washing, and one enters it with a bath given in the name of God. It is a community of baptized sinners who have hope of becoming saints, but not without Christ. There has always been sin in the church, and always shall be. It is especially obvious there because it is always in contradiction to its Lord. What keeps the church really the church is not the excellence of its members, but the continual renewal of the life and power of Christ within it.

The primitive church found that Christ was made known again in the Breaking of Bread. The early eucharist was the actualization of all that he was and did. It was not a mere repetition of the Last Supper, a fellowship meal of memorial, but an indescribably realistic communion with him in full resurrection joy. The body of Christ in eucharist made the body of Christ the church; Christians found their unity in him in the one loaf.

The early church was no mystery religion, a cult of myth without history. Its life centered in a concrete remembering, a perpetual recollection of Jesus. This was the source of the New Testament. It is the book which the church created and the book which creates the church.

The church obviously existed before the New Testament was written. Its earliest book dates a good twenty years after the resurrection. During that time the Gospel was preached and people believed by oral tradition. None of the books of the New Testament was written formally as "scripture." They were brought forth by situations which required letters, as in the case of the earliest writings, the epistles; or they were a gathering together of the deeds and sayings of Jesus and the stories of the earliest days, as they were remembered and used in liturgy and preaching. The last book of the New Testament, the Revelation of St. John the Divine, is a panoramic vision of the final destiny of the church and the world in the light of Christ, written to comfort the persecuted church.

The New Testament shows Jesus through the faith of the church. The books are passionate confessions of commitment to him. This is not objective reporting, it is enthusiastic propaganda. It is impossible to find a record of Jesus uncolored by what people said about him. There is no available Jesus except the Jesus of the earliest church. There is no way to know anything about him except through the writings which the church produced. The church creates the Gospel. The Gospel also creates the church. By it the people of God are constantly converted to faith and formed in life. The church increases literally by "evangelization," "gospelization." Correction and renewal of the church, which is one of the periodic characteristics of its life, comes from the return to the pattern of the New Testament.

Throughout the New Testament there is the emergence of a family life. The inescapable father figures of the apostles preside in strength and love. The principle that some are responsible for the faith of others is clearly accepted, for it comes from their appointment by Christ himself. As the Lord had said, those who receive the apostles are receiving him. The apostles hold their position not because of their goodness, administrative gifts—or infallibility—but because they had been given their commission by Jesus. Paul has to defend to the Galatians his designation as an apostle because it had come in a very special way from Christ in a vision.

The church of the New Testament thus has an emerging form in its common life. In the pattern discerned by Frederick Denison Maurice, it developed five "signs of a spiritual society": initiation in baptism, eucharistic worship, scripture, apostolic ministry, and common prayer. These visible signs have evolved in the course of history and their presence makes the church's organic community. They constitute the great continuities which keep creating its common life.

Commitment to Jesus leads to life in his church. There is no way of escaping this consequence if the Jesus of the New Testament is accepted in his entirety. Believing becomes a belonging: belonging in the body of Christ. Belonging *in* says it better than belonging *to*. Belonging *to* implies a kind of club with its roster of members. Belonging *in* the church means that you have, we each have, our rightful place in the family of God, where in Christ we belong. The gift of this membership means not only that we belong in the church, but the church belongs in us. It is ours, to serve us, to serve us in our faith.

To understand how the church serves us in believing we must have a fresh understanding of two words: *authority* and *tradition.* These two words are sorely in need of redemption, because their true meaning has been abused to the point of extinction.

Authority is present in the church. It is not something the church has, but is. Authority in this sense means "the right to speak." It must never be confused with power, the imposition of authority. This authority can never be imposed. Einstein is an authority in science. There is nothing threatening about this fact. My doctor is an authority in medicine. There is nothing threatening about that fact. Neither Einstein nor my doctor impose themselves on me. I go to them to find out, to learn, to be guided because of what they know.

The church is an authority in faith because I can find out from other Christians, and the life of Christ in them, what I could not possibly discover all by myself. I also find that the course of the history of this body leads me to believe that the Holy Spirit acts in it. One reason for this belief is simply that it seems impossible to think that there is no transcendent cause for the amazing consensus on the essential Christian doctrines across the centuries. The great instance is, of course, the creeds.

The Nicene Creed does not convince me because a group of ancient bishops voted for it in the fourth century under pressure from the Emperor. It does convince me because it gives the answer arising from Christian experience, and which the consensus of Christian experience has authenticated, to the question the Arian controversy provoked: does our salvation come from God or less than God? That answer which declares that Christ is God's own act, God's own presence, gloriously involved in human flesh, has satisfied the billions of holy common people of God each week at eucharist as they sing it. This impresses me, for that company includes every conceivable race and country, every degree of ignorance and education, every kind of culture. And year by year this faith in the Incarnation is celebrated at Christmas with a glow and joy that is ever contagious. I could never have thought up the doctrine of the Incarnation. It is mine because I belong in the church.

The church is a *tradition.* Tradition means a " handing on." It is an act of passing something from one person to another. It is what a father tells his child; it is a form of life. It is an act of giving directed toward the future; it is sharing what one has rather than keeping it for one's self—that is, when tradition is rightly used. Like authority, it is not something the church has, but is. It is a "handing on," a dynamic continuity.

When tradition is reversed it is evil. When it becomes a looking back, a fearful attempt to keep for oneself the old things which are comforting—when it is an attempt to assert superiority by a claim to antiquity—it is evil. But then it is not really tradition; it is not a form of life, but a form of death. Tradition is not forgetting. The church does not lose its memory, or if it does it ceases to be the church. The miracle of the memory of the church can be one of its greatest contributions in the modern age.

Tradition is a cure for amnesia. A "crisis of identity" is a commonplace of modern secular society. In fact, the society itself seems to suffer from it. Problems of identity often stem from loss of memory. One does not know who he is because he does not remember where he came from. This amnesiac pattern has been stimulated by the passion for the contemporary of a "now generation." The swiftness of change, the uprootings of a mobile population, the alienation between generations, the insecurity about meaning which concentration on the purely material and evanescent has produced—all of this has conspired to create a situation which could slowly destroy this culture.

Christian believing creates a belonging which helps to cure the "crisis of identity." The Christian finds that most intense strength from the great continuity of life which comes from the Living Christ in his members. This is the inner meaning of church history. This history belongs to the believer; he belongs to this history. To feel this it is necessary to approach the ages of Christianity with more imagination than the textbooks in church history. Not primarily in the great political struggles or in the influence of the church on culture and society is the witness to us to be found; it is in the faith, the energized life, the transformed societies, the beauty and the glory of twenty centuries that the testimony radiates.

Recovering the habit of pilgrimage is a way to stimulate Christian imagination about this living tradition. In a jet age how many millions go to Europe from America! It is not only in Jerusalem that we can find the holy place, *the place where* one can virtually feel holiness coming out of the ground. The catacombs, Assisi, the Canterbury of Thomas Becket. These are not simply tourist sites; they are *places where* the power of Christ can be almost tangibly sensed by the believer. The faith of other ages is visible too—who can stand unfeeling in the transfiguration of the windows of Chartres? And when we feel such places we are not experiencing a faith long past but our own faith in our own Christ. These epiphanies are not only beautiful but true.

Another way of revelation of the faith of other times comes through the history of Christian art. The paperback books of reproductions can serve as well as a European summer. Early Christian wall paintings, Byzantine icons, Romanesque sculpture. This also can be pilgrimage.

Every age has had an ability to perceive something about Christ that no other has seen. We have a bad habit of choosing golden ages—perhaps the age of the Fathers, the time of the Gothic glory, the Reformation—but every age has its proper testimony. All of this comes forth with vigor in the contributions of other centuries to liturgy and hymnody. We pray together with other ages, even in the same words. This is a form of family prayer as we eat at the same table of the Kingdom of God.

Belonging in the church means more than an historical membership. It is a great fellowship in the present. Ecumenicism has made this oneness active and real. For several decades churchmen have been occupied with the necessary task of trying to restore visible unity between Christian bodies. Too often this has been a work so preoccupied with resolving differences organizationally that it has come to naught. Quite rightly there is a reaction setting in against the kind of Christian unity which results in greater and greater corporations. Moreover, there has been a tendency to blur differences in conviction in the interests of unity. This has resulted in the curious phenomenon of schemes for unity which sometimes seem to be based on a diminution of faith. The enthusiasm for this kind of ecumenicism seems to be waning, but there is another kind of unity which should come first: a unity of shared faith and experience.

We live at a moment unrivalled for a thousand years for recovering a truly catholic consciousness by learning immediately from other Christians. During the centuries of separation, the Holy Spirit has revealed different aspects of Christ to each Christian confession. Now is the time for the re-integration of faith in the Lord as well as the re-integration of his church.

In my own imagination I see this in a pattern of the

Christian festivals and fasts. If I may have a fantasy of a year of Christian re-integration for myself, I would spend Advent with Scottish Presbyterians because of their sense of the sovereignty of God and Judgment; Christmas in an English Cathedral because of the Anglican feeling for the Incarnation; Epiphany with the Greek Orthodox because of the awareness of glory and transfiguration; Lent in the Benedictine or Cistercian abbey because of the practice of austerity; Holy Week in a German Lutheran congregation because of the great devotion to the sacrifice of the cross; Easter with the Russian Orthodox because of their joy in the resurrection, and Pentecost in a charismatic Roman Catholic parish because of its new feeling for the Holy Spirit. This would be an experience of catholicity which would be a revelation in faith. No matter what the canonical situation may be, all of these traditions belong to me, or rather I belong to them as I respond to Christ in them.

Belonging in the church—that means as Paul said: "all things are yours, whether Paul or Apollos or Cephas or the world or life or death or the present or the future, all are yours; and you are Christ's; and Christ is God's" (I Corinthians 3:21-23, RSV).

CHAPTER V

Knowing the Bible

The Bible is the book with the Presence in it. This is not a fact which can be demonstrated, but it can be experienced. It is a strange book which conveys such a sense of God that it has satisfied men in the most utterly different cultural backgrounds century after century. The French-American novelist Julien Green made an entry in his diary which reads:

Yesterday evening, I read the second chapter of the Epistle to the Ephesians. It contains this strange verse: '. . .and sins, wherein in time past ye walked according to the course of this world, according to the prince of the power of the air. . .' What echoes this rouses from the depths of the reader's soul! There are times — I hesitate to say so — when I resist a temptation to open the Bible, because I know the power of its spell. For me, it is far more than a book, it is a voice and a person.[11]

Not everyone senses the Presence and the voice in this book, the "power of its spell." This failure is not confined to non-Christians; it happens to Christians as well. Periodically there is a strong non-Biblical, if not anti-Biblical tendency within the church. We seem to be emerging from such a time. The Bible has been treated as a very valuable collection of ancient religious literature containing essential material about Jesus, but not necessarily normative for present day Christians. Even for liturgical worship other sources which show insight into the human situation have been given equal place. Since both the Old and the New Testaments are saturated with cultural presuppositions radically different from our own, they have been discounted as suspiciously irrelevant to our age. Why give ancient solutions to twentieth century problems?

In the face of this disparagement an opposite phenomenon has emerged which cannot be ignored: the increasing appeal of Biblical fundamentalism. By "fundamentalism" I mean the belief that the Bible is literally true; that it is necessary for a Christian believer to stifle all his reasonable questions about it, and accept it as divine dictation. This attitude has many variants, but at its heart there is the conviction that Christianity is just the religion of the book.

The attractiveness of fundamentalism comes from its reassuring definiteness. During the 1960's it was not uncommonly thought that the way to make the church effective and popular was to conform it more closely to the viewpoint of the modern world. When this kind of reduction has become dominant, there comes the inevitable question— what is the difference between the church and the world? Why do I have to be a Christian to believe that, to do that? In a time when people are becoming desperate for certainty, it is obvious that the religious positions which maintain the greatest distinctiveness, the highest definition, will have an increasing appeal.

The truth that one can believe in the Bible more deeply as the Word of God by accepting the most rigorous critical methods in studying it is in danger of getting lost. Part of the reason for this lies in the fact that for too many Biblical scholars the study of the scriptures had become merely a scientific puzzle. Their work was a careful examination of ancient documents, their history, composition, and translation, but it somehow avoided the question of theological truth.

A gap opened between the professional Biblical scholar

and the ordinary layman, even clergyman, who wanted to know what the texts meant for him. This had the disastrous result of separating the most careful Biblical learning from the common use of the scripture.

The most constructive Biblical development has come in the rapid appearance of great new translations of the Bible: *The Revised Standard Version, The Jerusalem Bible, The New English Bible, The American Bible,* and many others of lesser standing. With the life's work of hundreds of scholars behind them, they have made the text understandable in contemporary speech and have had a phenomenal acceptance. They have opened the scriptures again to modern folk.

A resistance to the new translations has understandably appeared. Nothing more normal could be expected than anxiety about what seemed like tampering with the holy language of the holy book. This anxiety seems to be in inverse ratio to a real knowledge of the Bible; it stems from a kind of fetishism about the book itself.

English-speaking Christians have a peculiar problem about new translations. The King James Bible is a classic of English literature. It has formed the language as well as the religion of the English-speaking world. The passage of centuries has given the archaic wording the sacred sound of a cultic language. How frequently it is forgotten—especially by those who call the version "The Saint James Bible"—that that translation sounded as modern when it first appeared as *The New English Bible* does now!

The language of the old English Bible is actually too good. It can now be venerated for itself, and in fact it is better language than the Hebrew and the Greek of the original. The holiness of the Bible is not to be conveyed by the smooth euphonious language, but by what it means. Is it also too much to say that part of the problem of the new versions is that the old language softens the impact of the word of God?

People are now reading the Bible as they have not read it for decades. In subways, on airplanes, it is common to see young people intently concentrating on a paperback of, say, the *Jerusalem Bible,* underscored heavily. They may be having a new experience of religion which their parents hardly believed possible. For them, as Julien Green said, ". . .it is far more than a book." The deep spiritual satisfaction they can find in it is something they will not relinquish. Some of them have been persuaded that they have to sacrifice their critical faculties to keep it. This is an unnecessary sacrifice, and an immoral one. One of the most imperative tasks of the church, a task for every priest, pastor, and teacher, is to show how the Bible can be known as the Word of God by those who really know all about it. That means knowing what it is, and what is in it.

What is the Bible? The Bible is a collection of books: sixty-six to be exact, thirty-nine in the Old Testament, twenty-seven in the New. The Old Testament books were written in Hebrew, the New Testament in Greek. Fifteen other books accepted as sacred by Greek-speaking Jews at the time of Jesus, called the Apocrypha, were composed during the time between the two Testaments and are at least para-Biblical. The obvious question so often never even asked about the Bible is—why these books?

The question is answered in the history of the very long discussion in the church out of which the canon emerged. "Canon" means rule or standard. "The canon of the scripture" means the standard list of books accepted as authentic sources for Christian faith. The list was not decided by church legislation; it grew. The question of the Apocrypha is an example of the nature of the problem. Is it, or is it not scripture? Most Christians in the world accept it in some sense as scripture; Protestants traditionally do not. This question was never finally settled to every Christian's satisfaction. It could be considered still open.

The process of settling what is and is not in the New Testament took over three hundred years. The writings which we know as the synoptic gospels, ten epistles of Paul, the Epistle to the Hebrews, and possibly the Acts of the Apostles, were the cluster of books generally acknowledged by 130 A.D. The rest were still under discussion until the fourth century, when the Eastern Church finally accepted the Revelation of St. John the Divine. This complicated story, of which there is as yet no final version, can be found in a good encyclopedia under the heading "Canon."

The Old Testament canon as it was accepted by Jews became part of the Christian canon because it was the scripture of Jesus and absolutely necessary to understand his life. To this it was also common to add the Apocrypha.

The Bible is then the book of the church. The church existed before the canon was formed, and the church in its common life determined the canon. This has the obvious corollary that the Bible is bound up with the life of the church.

Never does the Bible seem more what it is than when it is read and heard in the Christian liturgy. The common picture of the believer sequestered with his Bible in quietness and solitude is a false image. The truer image is that of the book being read *aloud* in the congregation and *heard* by the congregation, intent together on the reading. This is the proper context of the Bible, and even when the Christian reads it alone, he reads it as a member of the community in which it belongs. It is in the long history of the community that he finds the evidence of the authority and meaning of what he reads.

When Christians speak of the Bible as the Word of God, we mean that God speaks through the Bible. This book is not a collection of oracles, but a vehicle for God's communication of his self-revelation. It is not the book of the words of God, the dictations of the Deity. Behind the whole of this book is the Hebrew concept that God shows himself in his acts, he speaks in what happens in history. Also this speaking has to do with his people together. He does not communicate primarily through special illuminated individuals. The prophets of the Old Testament declare the word of God because they interpret the meaning of the events the whole nation was experiencing. His final communication, his final Word, is in the Word made flesh, in what happened through Jesus.

What is in the Bible? Stories, basically stories, and the meaning of those stories. The nucleus of the biblical material is essentially historical events. It is the tale of the working out of the purposes of God in "a history within history" which discloses him as he is.

The central story of the Bible is the Gospel. It is on the life of Jesus that the believer centers. Every now and then a person boasts that he has read the Bible from cover to cover, from start to finish. This *tour de force* is mistaken effort. The Old Testament is not what starts the scripture, but the New. It all has to be read in the light of Christ; in fact, at times expurgated in the light of Christ. That is not to say that the Old Testament is to be discarded, for it was the scripture of Jesus which spoke the word of God to him.

One of the most important functions of the Old Testament is to communicate to Christians what it communicated to Jesus: the realization that God is the living God, who reveals himself in history, not a principle or just an idea; the sense of living under the demanding gaze of a righteous God who requires justice in society, and speaks to his people through his prophets in judgment and hope; the assurance that God is a God of promise who enters into covenant relations that he will fulfill. These tremendous motifs are not only spelled out in narrative, prophecy, and wisdom literature; they are prayed out in the psalms, which were the prayer book of Jesus.

Modern people in the Western world, whose whole culture has been formed by the Bible to a greater extent than they realize, take for granted the idea of purposeful history. The awareness that history is going somewhere, in fact, that there is history at all, rather than recurring cycles or "one damn thing after another" without meaning is also an Old Testament creation. In the Old Testament there is no such thing as history out of control, because it is governed by God and has a destination.

In the second century, Marcion rejected the Old Testament because he believed the God of the Jews was another God from the God of Jesus Christ. This superficial heresy constantly returns. Much in the Old Testament needs purification in the light of the New, but the God of the Old Testament is the God of Jesus, and is the God of Christians. This God is not an idea but a Presence. This is the great difference between Greek philosophy and Hebrew religion, and between Greeks and Hebrews as types in every age. Christians are always Hebrews in this idea of God.

Christians are also Hebrews in their use of male imagery for God. The God of the Old Testament is always "he." Obviously, this does not mean that God is ever thought of as a male, and it does not signify male superiority. God is transcendent, he can never be identified with human characteristics, but he has to be spoken of in analogies to human experience. The God of the Bible, of both Testaments, is the God of divine initiative. He acts first, he is the One Who is begetter of his people, he is the generator of redemption.

There has never been a moment when the thought forms of any culture—including the cultures in which the Bible emerged—and the thought forms of the scripture are completely at one. Sometimes this comes from the fact that the world of the Bible is a more ignorant world than the world of a more sophisticated people. That was true of the Greeks and the Bible, and of ourselves and the Bible. When actual knowledge is at stake the Bible has to be corrected. However, "cultural conditioning" can be used as an excuse to erase the witness to moral and psychological differences between the Bible and twentieth century culture which are not a matter of knowledge but pertain to the image of God and man. In that issue the Bible has always been understood by Christians to be a corrective of any other world view. This has been the ground of prophetic protest in every generation against social injustice and moral degeneracy. In the name of removing what is "culturally conditioned," every element in the Bible that conflicts with modern man's world view and modern man's failure can be expurgated. The effect of this can be demonic.

More impressive than the "cultural conditioning" of the Bible is the evidence of the unconditioned in the Bible. This shows itself in the amazing way this book has made sense to people in the most diverse cultures. Twentieth century people are in danger of believing there is a real difference in kind between human beings now and in other ages. This sort of vanity has no basis in fact. Other cultures such as the Greek and the Oriental have had as radical differences from the Biblical world view as our own, yet the Bible has made sense in them, not by being assimilated, but by transforming them. Abraham, Isaac, and Jacob; Isaiah and Jeremiah; Peter and Paul; Jesus—all are friends and presences in Athens, Rome, in Chartres, in Bombay, and New York, wherever Christians live.

Paul is in the Bible. Being a Biblical Christian means coming to some sort of terms with this man. He had always proved a disturber of minds; people are likely to love him or hate him. He is as difficult for some Christians to assimilate as the Old Testament, and frequently for the same people.

Malcolm Muggeridge and Alec Vidler did a televised dialogue on Paul for the BBC on location from the sites of his journeys, and it was published under the title, *Paul, Envoy Extraordinary*. This book and the program on which it was based are one of several signs that there is a revived interest in the apostle. The book is prefaced by six pages of quotations of men who have venerated or despised him. These range from Ambrose — "Paul: Christ's second eye" — to Samuel Butler — "St. Paul would almost certainly have condemned tobacco if he had known of its existence." [12] This illustrated volume awakens the memory of the phenomenal physical achievement of this man's journeys, the overwhelming response to his mission in the Mediterranean cities, but most of all, the unique vocation he was given to shape the interpretation of the Christian faith for all time.

The writings of Paul are the earliest witness to Christian faith we possess; they antedate the gospels, whose position in the New Testament is logical, not chronological. His greatest importance, which is almost impossible to comprehend, lies in his decisive interpretation of the meaning of the life of Christ. It was his function to take the raw material of what he was told about Jesus and show what it ultimately means for faith. He did this in haste and in a fiery passion of belief, but it has formed the life of Christians ever since. "The Gospel according to Paul" is not genius; it is inspiration.

Knowing the Bible is not the same thing as knowing about the Bible. There is no substitute for incessantly reading the book. Christian believing comes from the constant intake of the scriptures. The metaphor of nourishment is the inevitable way of thinking of what the scripture does: it feeds the believer with the bread of the Word.

The beauty of this concept is in its implication—"we are what we eat." The Christian believer becomes a Biblical man. His life is sustained and energized by the scripture. This shows itself not in incessant, and even irritating, quoting of scripture, but in the way the meaning of his words, his vocabulary, his mind, are shaped. For instance, he knows that "love" is defined by the life of Jesus, that true love is not just desire but self-outpouring. He becomes a man who lives in the atmosphere of the Bible in which he expects God to act in history, his history. Quite simply, he is filled with the Word of God.

When Blaise Pascal, the seventeenth-century French lay theologian, one of the greatest of Christians, died, a servant found sewed in the lining of his coat a paper written in his own hand which contained a memento of a decisive mystical experience. Under a cross with rays and dated "In the year of grace 1654, Monday, November 23," it read:

From about ten-thirty in the evening to about
half an hour after
Midnight,
Fire.
God of Abraham, God of Isaac,
God of Jacob
not of the philosophers and savants,
Certitude, certitude; feeling, joy, peace.
God of Jesus Christ[13]

Pascal's words have become part of the spiritual heritage of

Christians. They reveal the meaning of being a Biblical Christian as no amount of discussion could disclose. This is the "voice" and the "person" of which Julien Green wrote three hundred years later. Christian believing comes, not by knowing about the Bible, but by knowing the Presence in it.

CHAPTER VI

Living Liturgically

The Christian liturgy is a way of life: it is a way Christians participate in the life of Christ, and a way Christ participates in the life of his church.[14] In the liturgy the Christian believer finds himself in the very presence of his Lord, actualized in time and space. This is the Christian mystery— but in what sense "mystery"?

The loss of a sense of mystery has become a common complaint against current trends in Christian worship. The revision of liturgical forms to make them intelligible to modern people has eliminated some romantic elements. The Latin of the Roman Mass is gone. The Elizabethan English of the Anglican Prayer Book is disappearing in the new rites. The updating of language has been accompanied by ceremonial changes incorporating the congregation into the liturgical action, and making every gesture plainly visible. Celebrating the eucharist facing the people has become standard practice, and the symbolic signs have been radically simplified.

Many a churchgoer has suffered shock from such changes. Sometimes the reaction has been close to "They have taken away my Lord, and I know not where they have laid him." The emotion is understandable, and sometimes justifiable when the transition has been abrupt, or characterized by unfeeling destruction, tastelessness, confusion, or outright vandalism of monuments of the past. Yet there is behind the objection too often a misunderstanding of the nature of the Christian mystery.

The Christian liturgy is a way in which Christians participate in the life of Christ. In this time of liturgical change this is still as true as ever and in many ways this transcendent mystery can become more powerful than before because it can be understood more easily.

Mystery, in the Christian sense, is never a darkening of meaning, but a revelation. It is never obfuscation, the enjoyment of the unearthly, the esoteric, or the obscure. There have been periods when it appeared that way. "Hocus-pocus" came from the Latin, *hoc est enim meum corpus,* the words of institution in the consecration of the Mass. The mystery of Christian worship does not depend on incantation, special language, or any effect humanly induced; it comes from the mystery inherent in God's action, the mystery of God himself. As we shall see in this book, this mystery is not dispelled by knowledge, but deepened by knowledge. Such is the mystery of the Christian liturgy.

The mystery of the liturgy is the Paschal Mystery. It is the glorious experience of entering into the redemption effected for us by Christ. It is the actualization, the making present, of Christ that we may enter into the power of his death and resurrection in union with him. This is mystery enough. It requires every kind of clarity to realize what it is. To comprehend it we must know what the Christian Passover is, for this is the Passover (Paschal) Mystery.

Jesus went up to Jerusalem deliberately at the Passover because that feast was essential to his purpose. The Passover was the annual commemoration of God's deliverance of Israel out of Egypt. It recalled the passing over, by the angel of death, of the houses of God's people, and his smiting the Egyptians' first-born sons. It celebrated the Exodus which this terrible plague made possible. This was the feast of the release of Israel, of God's bringing Israel out of Egypt into the Promised Land.

Deliberately at this time, Jesus went through his own Exodus. Knowing the inevitable consequences of his challenge to Jerusalem, he chose the Passover as the moment for his passage from life, through death, to life again. This Exodus of Jesus would be the action whereby God again gives his people—now his new people—this final deliverance. The Jewish Passover was understood to be more than a mere memorial; it was a participating in the Exodus itself. All this meaning lies behind the church's understanding of its liturgical action. It is the significance of baptism and the eucharist.

In the New Testament church baptism was understood as entering into this Paschal Mystery: "In baptism you were buried with him, in baptism also you were raised to life with him through your faith in the active power of God who raised him from the dead" (Colossians 2:12). The power of this act was visibly symbolized by actual immersion—burial in water. This great sacramental sign has now degenerated to a mere token. Baptism was not finished and done by this immersion; the mystery was present ever after. The Christian lived by "faith in the active power of God" which had been given him in his initiation.

The eucharist is the regularly renewed experience of the Paschal Mystery. When Jesus instituted this sacrament at the Last Supper, he determined, then and there, by what he did with the bread and wine, the meaning of what he was about to do with his body and blood. By choosing the Passover as the occasion, he designated his passion to be the New Passover, the New Exodus, the New Deliverance for the whole world. This saving act was to be accomplished by his sacrificial death and God's response to it.

In a real sense what followed after the Supper instituted the eucharist. He went through it all, as he had acted it out in symbolic signs. Calvary and the Empty Tomb become the Passover of Christ. Calvary and the Empty Tomb are the institution of the eucharist. The Last Supper would be nothing without them; indeed the Last Supper was not a eucharist, but the provision for the eucharist. The purpose of Christ's action at the Last Supper was to make his death and resurrection available to his disciples thereafter.

Jesus did not institute a new rite; he reinterpreted an old one. The eucharist does not come from a new ritual act; the ritual act was already there—a common meal of his disciples, a bread and wine ceremony in some way connected with the Passover. Even after his death it would go on so long as his disciples stayed together. He did not need to tell them to keep doing this afterward. What he did tell them was something they could never understand until it was all over—or better, until it had begun. He told them what henceforth the bread and the wine and the meal were to be: they were to be his Presence, they were to be for the re-calling—for the calling back of him. Why did he do this? The answer to this question can be found in the sacramental experience of a Christian congregation.

For over a decade I was rector of a town church which stood on a slight rise of land. On summer Sundays, when there was more time between services, I found it pleasant to stand outside the door as the congregations entered. From the vantage point of the church steps I could see the people coming each from his own somewhere. I stayed in the parish long enough to know what many of them left as they closed their doors and came. I knew what they brought with them, in them. In my imagination I see this as a procession, a real liturgical procession, which the church in that place made week by week. They came, not just to "church," but to the altar, to the eucharist. They took what they brought of problems, weakness, sins, to the place of the Body and Blood and then returned—another procession. They returned, but it was different, and that is why they kept coming, week by week and year by year, in this slow rhythmical pattern that has kept creating the church since the resurrection. What does this memory, which every priest has in some form, really mean?

The eucharistic rhythm to and from the Table means that at the Table there is something to be found that is nowhere else. It is the transforming, energizing presence which Christ gave his church through the Last Supper. This is not just a subjective intellectual or emotional presence. It is a meeting, an appointment, if you will, that Christ has made with us. And in every generation for nineteen hundred years, people keep coming back because something has happened to them through this understanding Christ has with his church.

The ways in which Christians have understood what happens have varied, and the history of trying to define it is depressing, but the most important affirmation which the Church Eucharistic makes is that Christ happens to those who gather at the Table.

For a while now we have been involved in the wonderful task of recovering a more real and adequate sense of the eucharist as the common meal of the body of Christ, but in the process we may now be losing the Christ in the common meal. In the liturgical movement we have learned that this sacrament is a corporate action, something that Christians do, not just something done to them or for them. This has resulted in a tremendous improvement in the vitality of worship. The individualism of a private *"tête-à-tête* with Jesus" piety at the Holy Communion is disappearing. We know that the liturgy is not a form of words to be said or read, but basically a deed done together. Folk masses, rock masses, all kinds of experiments have been tried to bring people into the action more effectively.

The meaning of bread and wine have again come clear. There elements represent our life together, our selves, our souls and bodies, our jobs, our families, our economy, our society. We know that in offering them we symbolically bring all this to the altar.

The eucharist has again become a fellowship meal. We gather closely around the altar; we actually eat and drink—real bread, loaves: bread that is crusty and good to eat; and red wine, enough really to drink. This is good.

Sometimes we come to this point of understanding and stop. We have such an intense sense of fellowship and warmth, and this is such a radically different feeling from the old stuffy church ways that we stop there. We think we have rediscovered the eucharist, and perhaps the church. But the giving of the Peace can sometimes mean more than the Communion.

A peculiar sectarianism has also come into the church in the name of corporate participation in the liturgy. The liturgy for the congenial, cohesive small group can be an intense experience; it can also be a great temptation for unintentional schism. The hazard is particularly present now because our depersonalized society has created such a desperate need for human togetherness. The church must satisfy this need but never permit the development of subjective emotionalism to corrupt the liturgy. When small liturgical groups come to believe that the effectiveness of the eucharist can be measured by its psychological dynamics, the liturgy is in danger of becoming a Dionysian happening. This lies behind many of the problems Paul had to deal with in Corinth.

For instance, is the eucharist "the celebration of life"?

This slogan has had great popularity. With a memory of the deadness and dreariness of conventional services, the phrase is appealing, but the trivial "liturgical" activity it has generated can have an unholy ambiguity. "Celebration of life"—whose life? Mine? Yours? Life does not come in general; it comes in particular. Do we go to the table to celebrate what we are, how we live? Is the communion we share a communion of the bread and wine of our selves? Or are we the problem for which the eucharist is the solution? The eucharist is not "the celebration of life," it is the celebration of Christ! It is his life, not ours, we celebrate!

What the church needs to recover at this moment is the realization of itself as the great eucharistic church. Sometimes it comes in wonderful ways. It can be vivid to a priest who communicates an Easter congregation, if he is not too fatigued for imagination. The multitude of the unfaithful people of God being formed again into the body of Christ by the resurrection! The priest, if he is the pastor of this congregation, also knows the strange companions gathered together at the Table. People who could never make a "community" in any social sense meet side by side for their communion. This is the reality of the church.

One Pentecost I was in Notre Dame in Paris. Ten thousand people there sang the Mass with amazing vigor. The building participated too, for the testimony of centuries of French life, of Christian life, was gloriously present. Very important to me was the fact that I could not quite understand the words with my rather pathetic French. These people were not my people, and yet they were. Never have I felt the reality of the eucharistic church more fervently than in that multitude, not one of whom I knew, because we were all known by the Christ in whom we were made into the family of God.

The eucharist is a way by which Christ participates in his church. The bread which we bring to the altar representing ourselves is en-Christed. It is then given back to us full of him. The chief actor in the eucharist is Christ, who is Lord of the Table. He is really present. What this means can best be perceived by asking the question, "What is the eucharist for?"

If it means the actualizing of the death and resurrection of Jesus, then the question, "What is the eucharist for?" becomes the question, "What is Christ for?" Quite simply, he is for the needs of men. His eucharist is surely for the sick, the depressed, the senile. It is for the dying, those condemned to die, the battlefield. In short, it is for those human situations when men are not only not at their best, but often past feeling and thinking. Christ has to have a means of reaching them. That is the reason he has this covenant with his church, that no matter what the psychological or the physical conditions may be, when it does this with bread and wine, then it is his body, it is his blood. He concretizes himself to meet us, whatever our condition. This is the sacramental expression of "the scandal of particularity." And because he is there for our uttermost need, he is there for our uttermost joy.

The eucharist is also the great sacrament of absolution. Jesus Christ came to save sinners. His body and blood are for the remission of the sins of the whole world. Granted that at the Reformation and in Protestantism this became the exclusive emphasis, and our rites need to be expanded to include "all other benefits of his passion," but this is no reason for reaction. There should always be a penitential preparation for communion, for the communion is not for the good and the worthy but the guilty. That preparation need not be during the celebration itself, but can be before.

What is needed is more, not less, personal and corporate confession of sin, and even more deliberate preaching, teaching, of forgiveness. No one knows the joy of the eucharist until he finds in it the joy of a cleansed life.

The eucharist also is an empowering, and a sending out. There is great good sense in sending the congregation out as soon as possible after the communion. The Christian has received strength to do more than he can: to do all things through Christ who strengthens him. Eucharist is not finished in church. The church receives the body of Christ at the Table to go out to be the body of Christ in the world.

"This wonderful sacrament" transforms the whole of life into the festival of Christ. For every joy and every sorrow, for weddings and for burials, for the routine and dreary succession of our weeks, for moments when we are "surprised by joy"—this is Christ's appointed means of transfiguring them all!

The eucharist is a way of life; of Christ's life and our life interacting day by day and year by year. It becomes "the sanctification of time." In the course of centuries time has been made holy by the liturgy through a temporally articulated ministry of the Word. This is perhaps the best way of understanding the Church Year.

The liturgical seasons are more than a scheme for religious education, a kind of dramatic playing out of the Gospel. They are a form of the real presence of the Word. Christ is proclaimed and present, to be received in this wonderful way by which we can live his life through with him. At Christmas and at Easter the sense of really "being there" is so intense that it even filters into the secular society. "The Christmas spirit" becomes a luminous, momentary means of redemption, and the resurrection joy at Easter even permeates the rites of spring, no matter what we say.

In this pattern the fast is as important as the feast. The eve of the feast is a fast. Advent, Lent, all the rest—the significance of these times is easily lost if we forget that the Christ of the eucharist is *in* but not *of* the world. There is a place for Christian world denial as much as for Christian world affirmation. In a consumer culture the sign of fasting has to be a means of identifying the Christian.

A Christian believer is thus not just thinking of Jesus, but in a marvelous way which is also part of the Christian mystery, meeting him with the church. The Lord's life is spread out again in time—lived year after year. Whole cultures have sensed this in the past and lived by a Christian rhythm. This could happen again.

The Christian liturgy is a means by which Christ penetrates the world with his redeeming action. He does this by entering his church again and again in perfectly predictable ways. It is a form of his faithfulness, by which, having loved his own, he loves them unto the end. Christian believing becomes through the liturgy participating in Christ, being drawn into the body of Christ in which we "evermore live in him and he in us."

CHAPTER VII

Thinking Theologically

Theology means "the knowledge of God." Christians believe that theology is possible, that it is possible to know God. A Christian believer is a theologian in that starkly simple sense when the knowledge of God comes to him through faith.

The word "theology" does not necessarily evoke this obvious yet awful meaning. It has come to sound academic and professional. What is a theologian? A man who knows God? If so, perhaps it would be better for someone to say that *about* him, rather than for him to say it about himself! Such caution does not seem to deter anyone in the use of the term. "Death-of-God theologian" and "atheistic theology" enjoyed currency in a recent fad. Such weird contradictions in terms signify a final stage in decomposition of meaning. It comes from the process of shifting from theology as the knowledge of God, to theology as knowing about God, to theology as knowing what others know, or do not know, about God. Finally, theology becomes a sort of objective, academic concern, a generalized study of anything pertaining to religion. The implication is that this is all that is now left of what used to be confidently considered "the knowledge of God."

It is not surprising that many people do not expect much from theology and theologians in the present state of affairs, and turn to any and every other source which offers religious satisfaction.

The church need not wait for the professor of theology to become again a man of faith to discover the reality of theology. Time and again in Christian history the theological service of God has been performed by the common people of God. Such a time may have come again.

Christian theology is the knowledge of God that comes from Christian believing; that is, it makes sense out of the confession of faith, "Jesus is Lord," and what that means about God. This is the way to recover Christian theology. The God whom we know is the God who gives us Christ! He is not just an abstraction, the object of speculative proof.

It is impossible to imagine Jesus trying to prove God's existence. Such "proofs" are not the beginning of Christian theology. They might seem to be the first obvious step, but proofs of God's existence have never made a believer. There are many intelligent ways of arguing that God is, yet it is clear that they do not compel belief. The best logician is not the most convinced theist. The most this exercise of "proof" demonstrates is that it is not unreasonable to believe in God. The whole project is shaky, not because of faulty reasoning, but because it considers God as a provable being. Even human beings are not provable beings. It is actually impossible for me to prove to anyone else that I exist. The provable God has a way of turning out to be an abstraction: the Unmoved Mover, the First Cause, the Absolute, or in popular terminology, "the Supreme Being." He (or It) is not the God and Father of our Lord Jesus Christ.

God has been in question for some time, even among Christians. Many questions have been asked about him within the church which used to be asked only outside. Is the Biblical image of God still viable? Does God exist? Does "God-talk" make sense? "The debate about God" has frightened many Christians, not only because it seemed faithless and negative, but also because they are not really used to thinking about God at all. They have taken God for granted. "The debate about God" has actually served a purpose because it has forced us to think about him again. It has centered attention on God, and dreadfully disturbed our inadequate patterns of thinking and talking about him.

How easily all of us break the Third Commandment! Pious people who would be horrified at profanity can take the name of God in vain by speaking of him in silly and superficial ways. It is always a risky business to talk about God. Take, for instance, the hazard in dealing with the elemental question, "Does God exist?"

A Christian means by "God" what Jesus meant. God is worshipful, holy, the Creator to be obeyed and to be loved, the transcendant Lord over all. Now listen to the careful words of the eighth-century Church father, John of Damascus:

God is infinite and incomprehensible, and all that is comprehensible about Him is His infinity and incomprehensibility. . . .God does not belong to the class of existing things: not that He has no existence, but that He is above all existing things, nay even above existence itself.[15]

God is beyond existence. This is a better way to put it than Tillich's phrase "the Ground of Being," which had such currency as a slogan. God is the source of existence, not an *existent*. He is beyond being. This is the awful mystery of transcendence. It means that God is not one item among all the items of existence. If by some supernal marvel there should be an infinite computer that could give the ultimate list of the multitude of things there are in existence, and if God were left out of that list, would it be one item short? No. God is not that kind.

We have no adequate words to define God; in the deepest sense we never can imagine him, for all our language, all our images, are made of the Creation which he is beyond. He is, as the prophets knew, the Hidden God, the God who dwells in thick darkness. The mystery of God is inexpressible. To think God is to think the unthinkable. How, then, can that be done? How can one know the Hidden God?

The knowledge of God in Christian theology comes not from speculation about him, but from union with him. We cannot explore his inner nature, but we can enter into communion with him. This experience reaches its supreme moment when God comes to us in Jesus. The kind of knowledge that belongs to the believer is the kind of knowledge that one has of a person.

God is a mystery, and our knowledge of him is knowing a mystery. There are two kinds of mystery: the kind that is like a secret, and the kind that is like a person. The mystery of a secret is like a mystery story. When "whodunit" is known, the mystery is gone. This is not so in the mystery of a person. The more we know the person, the more the mystery deepens. This mystery is never exhausted by knowledge, but becomes more fascinating. This is the way it is with knowing the inexhaustible mystery of God.

The knowledge of God is like the highest ways of human knowing. When God comes to us in Christ, he does not deliver himself to us in the generality of a philosophical abstraction, but in the particularity of a person. The only way to know a person is by faith—faith understood as trust. You can never come to know anyone by inspection, by investigation, but only by a relationship of trusting faith. This is the theological pattern. Faith precedes knowledge. We know God by trusting him, by committing ourselves to him. The words of Anselm are everlastingly true: "I believe, in order that I may know." This is risky.

I have an acquaintance who is working in the field of sociology of games. He intends to do a study of gambling. Recently he said to me, "You know, there is a similarity between gambling and religion." I asked him what that was. He said: "Risk."

Christians take the risk of faith, not out of curiosity, but out of need. The faith which gives the knowledge of God is a saving faith. When God shows himself to us, he does so in action on our behalf. He comes to us as Saviour. The awful dimensions which this implies are gathered up in the name "Christ," which we apply to Jesus.

"Jesus Christ" is a confession of faith. The term "Christ" has a definite meaning. It is not the surname of Jesus, as our casual use might imply, nor does it simply mean "great spiritual example," as the common term "Christ-figure" seems to indicate. There is no other Christ than Jesus for a Christian, for "Christ" means the Expected One, the Deliverer. The word is the Greek *Christos,* the Anointed, which was in the New Testament use equivalent for Messiah. It is as the Christ that Christians know Jesus.

The saving action of God in Jesus which "Christ" signifies is the means whereby we know what God is like. To put it directly: the redemption is the revelation. We do not look at Jesus and think, "What a beautiful person! Surely God is like Jesus!" Rather, we conclude from what happened in Jesus, in the totality of his life, his death, his resurrection, that God alone could have done this. We reach this conclusion because what these mighty acts do for us is restore our own relation to God.

The redemption is the revelation—redemption from what? Our knowledge of God is strangely involved with our sin. Sin is a theological concept, not a moral one. It does not mean the infraction of a standard of conduct, but the alienation, the lostness, the contamination which a fallen creature feels in the presence of the Holy God who is his Creator. A sense of sin grows simultaneously with a sense of God's self-disclosure. In fact, it reaches its height—or depth—with the awareness of the contrast between our self-centeredness and the love of God in Christ. The gap between us and God is the measure of his forgiveness and our salvation. God has done something about this condition. He has acted when we could not redeem ourselves. This is the joyful discovery. But this action is not simply "out there"; it is *in here,* in the inmost center of my being. Salvation means health, healing, wholeness; not as something else than forgiveness, but as the consequence of forgiveness.

The Christian experience of salvation is the way into the great question of the nature of Christ, of Christology. A commonly expressed mistake is to state that such ideas as the doctrine of the Incarnation in the Nicene Creed and its development into the Trinity were the work of Greek philosophers speculating theologically, and can mean nothing to a simple Christian, or certainly a modern man of the twentieth century. Actually these doctrines are the victory of the faith of the common man.

The process of development of Christian faith involves conflict. A dogma, that is, a Christian belief arrived at by the corporate consent of the church is set forth normally only when there is deep disagreement threatening the faith of common Christians, as in the Arian dispute, which occasioned the Nicene Creed. Furthermore, the result comes not so much from the testimony of theological specialists as from the ordinary devotion of Christians. *Lex orandi lex credendi.* "The rule of prayer is the rule of belief." The liturgical forms especially pertain to this process.

The doctrine of the Incarnation was the victory of the faith of the common man against the speculations of the philosophers, rather than vice versa. The mind of Arius represented the Greek sophisticate's desire to avoid the idea of God in the flesh by making Christ a kind of unearthly demigod. God in the flesh was and is a notion abhorrent to the classical Greek philosophical mind. It is a *scandal.*

The doctrine of the Trinity of God is likewise a *scandal.* This most profound and paradoxical of doctrines offends the philosophical mind because it has the apparent contradiction of the One who is Three at the heart of it. The Trinity is the consequence of affirming the Incarnation, even though it introduces a complexity in the life of God, by bravely being willing to take the experience of the Spirit at its face value as a divine manifestation, for in his renewing, creating, and sanctifying action, he is doing what only God can do.

What kind of knowledge of God do such doctrines indicate? First and foremost, it is the knowledge which comes from experience, the kind of knowledge which comes from the experience of persons. We know him in whom we have believed; but we know him together, for the experience is corporate, in the common life of the church. The experience is not just individual experience; in fact, it is dangerous to theologize alone. This has been demonstrated in the classic case of Dietrich Bonhoeffer, who wrote the enigmatic letters from prison, so fascinating, so intriguing, that they enticed great bodies of churchmen into believing that they were a new revelation. We are now in the process of radical revision of the "secularization of Christianity," because events have proved false his predictions of a non-religious future, and the inevitable call to speak in a non-religious fashion about God.[16]

Theology is practical knowledge. The knowledge of God cannot be kept separate from living. It is only in the past three hundred years that the notion of separating theology and ethics appeared; the early books on Christian belief included the treatment of Christian behavior. Christian ethics is simply the working out of Christian belief in practice. My great teacher, Richard Niebuhr, used to make this plain in his famous course on Christian Ethics. He taught it by drawing the theological implications from theology: the ethics of creation, the ethics of redemption, and so on. It was an articulation of the consequences which Christian believing has for making judgments and decisions in the human situation. All Christian ethics is theological ethics.

It may seem far-fetched to think of some Christian doctrines as having an ethical application. What is the ethical consequence of the doctrine of the Trinity, for instance? Anyone who has read Charles Williams' books knows that he bases his novels and his essays on the idea of "coinherence," which he derives from the Trinity of God. The Many in the One is the principle of the life of the Trinity. Man is made in the image of God and participates in that principle. We all therefore "coinhere," live in each other. This became the great inspiration for his deep intuitions of that it means to bear one another's burdens. Or again, to quote from a young English scholar who is now a priest of the Orthodox Church:

Our social programme, said the Russian thinker Fedorov, is the dogma of the Trinity. Orthodoxy believes most passionately that the doctrine of the Holy Trinity is not a piece of "high theology" reserved for the professional scholar, but something that has a living, *practical* importance for every Christian. Man, so the Bible teaches, is made in the image of God, and to Christians God means the Trinity: thus it is only in the light of the dogma of the Trinity that man can understand who he is and what God intends him to be. Our private lives, our personal relations, and all our plans of forming a Christian society depend upon a right theology of the Trinity. "Between the Trinity and Hell there lies no other choice." As an Anglican writer has put it: "In this doctrine is summed up the new way of thinking about God, in the power of which the fishermen went out to convert the Greco-Roman world. It marks a saving revolution in human thought." [17]

Or again, now that ecology is such a necessary concern for the future of the human race, is there a theology of ecology? The doctrine of creation means that the earth is the Lord's. God himself came to man in human flesh, which shows that the union of materiality with him is his purpose, and that he intends to save the world in more than a spiritual fashion. Destroying the environment is thus a violation of the will of God. When man pollutes the earth, it is, therefore, more than a mistake to be corrected; it is a sin which God judges, and for which human beings are ultimately accountable. But most of all, a Christian believer loves the earth because he can see the world reverently, as a sacrament of God's self-giving, for through his creation he can be known and found.

Thinking theologically results in action. Real theology produces deeds. Christian faith is a gift, a gift like the "talents" in the parable of Jesus. If we try to hide it in a field, it is taken away. It is only when we put it to use that the Lord is satisfied. In fact, if it is not at work, it disappears. Part of its working is very explicit sharing.

Believing results in witness. There is no such thing as faith which is not confessed before men. We do not have the saving knowledge of God in order to satisfy our private curiosity. Does this mean that a Christian tries to convert people? Is that not an invasion of other people's privacy, an act of spiritual imperialism?

Twice I have been to Europe alone. Both times these trips were experiences of frustration, for I saw much that excited

me but there was no one with me to share the discovery—
"Come here and see this!" Have you ever known a person to
be passionate about Bach or a rock group, and keep it to
himself? Have you ever become devoted to a great teacher
and held it within yourself?

Such considerations make the proper context in which to
consider Christian witness. It is shared discovery, shared joy.
Aggressive proselytizing is different in kind; it becomes a
revolting parody which convinces nobody. But keeping the
knowledge of God to oneself is unthinkable.

Should a Christian try to convert a non-Christian? Are not
all religions means of knowing God? Is the Christian faith the
only true faith? The questions seem strangely disturbing now.
Most Christians appear peculiarly unaware of the one
Christian conviction which directly pertains to the answers:
Jesus Christ is the *Logos,* the Word of God, "the real light
which enlightens every man" (John 1:9). The Incarnation is the enfleshment of all that is true, in Jesus. To put it
the other way round, Jesus is the light which shows what is
true in every faith. Surely the American Indian religions and
Hinduism have truth in them, and it is not necessary or even
honest to deny it. This can be appropriated, baptized, if you
will, into Christian life. It has happened a million times, and
still happens. But there are points of conflict which a real
study of comparative religion will reveal. In that case,
nothing which diminishes or contradicts the revelation of
God in Christ can be acceptable. Remember this: there would
have been no Christian faith unless somebody had convinced
somebody else originally. In the deepest sense the actual
conversion is God's business, but the witness is ours. If the
resurrection is real and the Incarnation is true, every
Christian believer is sent to proclaim Christ by what he says
and how he lives.

To be a witness is to be convincing. There is a theological discipline called "apologetics." The word, because of a change of language has an unfortunate sound. It does not mean making excuses for Christian belief, but presenting it so that it can be believed. The Greek word, *apologia,* signifies an explanation or a defense of a position.

The basic work of apologetics is internal; one has to convince himself. This produces a constant dialogue within a Christian's mind which he should never fear nor shirk, because what he believes has to be related to the experiences and the truth that come into him from every side. This means developing an apologetic habit of mind of relating Christian believing to everything that happens. This requires the development of an open but critical sense of the culture around us which becomes a part of us, like the air we breathe. It also means being sensitive to the changing patterns of the world, not gullibly assuming their goodness because they are new and fascinating, nor rejecting them because they have never happened before. It is a task which requires a Christian to become utterly alert and alive to the world in which he is living. The encounter between faith and the cultures of mankind has been the cutting edge of theology. As the witness has been given to one culture after another, theology has developed and deepened its insights and expression. This is the task of the modern church in America as well as of the Greek church in ancient Athens.

Witness can be costly. The word *martyr* is the Greek word for witness. It means theology with blood on it. The knowledge of God comes through a cross, and it is not surprising that Christians make this sign both liturgically and in life. A Christian himself is supposed to be a sign of contradiction because he knows something about God and man that the world rejects. It is dangerous not to be conformed to the world but to be transformed by the renewing of our minds, which is what theology is. When believing "Jesus is Lord" is in conflict with society, some-thing—even something fatal—can happen. This is always the test of the sincerity of our belief. It is also the most persuasive witness.

Christian believing requires thinking theologically. This is more than an intellectual experience but never less than one. As the theologian Jaroslav Pelikan has put it: "The church is more than a school. . . .But the church cannot be less than a school."[18] The intellectual experience of Christ is as real and necessary as mystical or moral experience of him. This is a truth the church may be in the process of losing as it absorbs more and more of the anti-intellectualism, if not irrationality, of our culture. If this happens the church will not only lose its mind but its soul. The theological failure of the church at this time is one of the ways it has by-passed human need. People are now in as much need of meaning, as of physical, economic, and political help. Christ calls us at this moment not only to feel and to act, but to think, and then to speak. The church must again become the teaching church. The Spirit is stirring in the church, and he is the Spirit of truth. He can stir minds as well as hearts!

CHAPTER VIII

Praying Continually

A Christian believer prays. He prays because he is a human being, and it is humanly natural to pray. He prays because he has been taught to pray by Jesus, both by his example and by his words. He prays because he *can* pray through Jesus Christ his Lord.

Such assumptions have been taken for granted throughout the whole history of the church, but they have lately become unclear to some Christians. "The crisis of spirituality" has developed as a consequence of "the crisis of faith." As a result, large numbers, not only of laymen, but of priests, ministers, and members of religious orders, openly and unashamedly, admit that they no longer pray.

In accounting for this predicament, it is constantly said that "the old ways don't work any more." By "the old ways" are meant the methods of devotion with which the previous generation grew up, or perhaps were the practices in seminaries during the mid-century.

Browsing in a bookshop recently, I picked up a small volume called *Searching for Icons in Russia* by Vladimir Solukhim[19]. The author, a young Russian, told of his excitement the first time he saw a really old icon divested of its layers of paint. So obscured by varnish were these old paintings that they were called, simply, "black boards." As he watched an artisan remove several coats of varnish, the young man suddenly saw a colorful picture begin to emerge, and his excitement was boundless. The artisan informed him, however, that what they had come to was merely an overpainting. This he also removed, and he kept working until at last was revealed the original icon, serene and glowing.

This can be a parable of our predicament. The over-painting of the original may be the "old ways" which "no longer work." There is reason to believe this, since so much of the spirituality and prayer talked about seems to be joyless, centering on the discipline of it, on prayer by rule and by rote, on prayer in terms of asking and getting. It seems to imply that praying is, for a believer, something for special times and, since these special times seem unreal or difficult, therefore for no time. All this is in such contrast to the intensive prayer of Jesus and the jubilant prayer of the saints that something original has obviously been overlaid.

When we take a careful look at the "old ways," they are often found in books on prayer and private devotion which were based on religious movements of the past hundred years. Some of these were romantic in mood, even attempt-ing to revive the methods of medieval piety. A priest friend of mine said he had received his seminary training in the High Middle Ages. He had been trained as an Anglican in a tradition which deliberately sought to reproduce the glories of that piety in the modern age. The problem is not that the way was old—the Middle Ages were only five hundred years ago—but that it was not old enough.

Ressourcement, as the French say—going back to the sources—is a sure principle of renewal. Sometimes we find that other traditions, such as the Eastern Orthodox, have preserved principles of spiritual life that are so old that they are new to us. They are in fact the vehicles by which elements of original Christian religion have been transported through the centuries direct to us.

If special times and places for prayer seem unreal, the alternative does not have to be no time at all, or just impulsive prayer; there is the New Testament principle of Paul—"pray continually" (I Thessalonians 5:17). This is the really old way, the original icon: prayer as a continuing state of life, a kind of being. Eastern Christianity has a specific technique for unceasing prayer, called the Prayer of Jesus. The small classic in spirituality, *The Way of a Pilgrim*[20] has made it known to thousands of Western Christians. In this diary, a simple, unknown Russian peasant of the early nineteenth century tells of the adventure of soul on which he embarked. When his wife died, he began a walking pilgrimage from holy place to holy place, in quest of an answer to the question: How can a Christian follow the injunction of the apostle Paul to "pray continually?" At last he came across a learned and patient monk who told him to use the Prayer of Jesus. This is simply saying over and over again the words, "Lord Jesus Christ, Son of God, have mercy on me, a sinner." It was to be done a few times only at first—only three thousand a day—but eventually synchronized with the vital rhythm of breathing. Finally, it would become a part of the unconscious pattern of his life, sinking deeply below the level of concentration to become one with his inner self. Then the prayer would pray in him.

The monk taught him these things, and also gave him a tattered copy of the classic collection of writings on the Prayer of Jesus called the *Philokalia.* The pilgrim went his way, to experience the deepening satisfaction of praying continually until finally the prayer prayed in him.

Franny and Zooey, a novel by J. D. Salinger, made all of this popularly known a few years ago. Franny is a Vassar student who is simultaneously getting religion and a nervous breakdown. The religion is coming from *The Way of a Pilgrim* and the Prayer of Jesus, which she is trying to practice as a sort of esoteric mystery. Her brother Zooey—they were both

"Quiz Kids" of a certain kind of miraculous intelligence—has a memorable encounter with her, telling her that the way out of her nervous trouble is not in a religion of escape, for which she is using her prayer, but in the kind of realism that is in Jesus. She has to know to whom she is praying. It has to be the real Jesus. She has just got him all confused with Heidi's grandfather. She has to recover the Jesus of the gospels.

Unceasing prayer is a concept which could prove to be a breakthrough in the problem of modern spirituality. Many of the efforts to provide a new spirituality in the secular fashion seem to demonstrate the problem more than provide the solution, because they participate so pathetically in the impoverished self-understanding of contemporary man. They are a demonstration of one-dimensional soul without any sense of otherness. It is not surprising that young people turn to the oriental religions for insight.

Praying continually with such a prayer as the Prayer of Jesus implies that prayer is a state of being, of being in God. This prayer is a *mantra,* such as is used in Eastern religions: a form of words to be repeated over and over again because it has an infinite capacity for meaning. The Orthodox were in contact with the East long before we were, and their experience in baptizing religious techniques is all available to us. We do not have to start the process for the first time. A *mantra* said or sung has as its purpose inducing a condition of spiritual existence. It is a method which shows that truth which the East can always tell the West: being has to precede doing.

The Prayer of Jesus is a Christian *mantra.* As Zooey told Franny, whom you are talking to makes all the difference. The Christian is speaking to Christ, he is *being in Christ.* The pilgrim carried two books: the Bible and the *Philokalia.* He read the Gospel as well as the book about the prayer. The unceasing liturgical use of the phrase "through Jesus Christ our Lord" in prayer also signifies something; it is not just a stock phrase to give warning at the end of a prayer that an "Amen" is in the offing. It expresses the condition of all prayer—being in Christ.

The ground of Christian prayer is the Lordship of Christ. The crucified and Risen Saviour who has taken our humanity into God in his glorified life is our Mediator. He is the one always with us and always with God. He is the Living, the Present Christ in whom we live and with whom we constantly are in communion. This makes the essential unity between personal and liturgical prayer. All true prayer is eucharistic because it is this act of communion with Christ. The purpose of Christian prayer before all else is to actualize this oneness with God through him.

The Prayer of Jesus comes in many forms. Its primitive practice may just have been the invocation of the very name of "Jesus." It expanded in expression with use. For centuries it has contained the words, "have mercy on me, a sinner." The penitential tone may put off some people, particularly those who need it most. It may well be that one essential problem in the crisis of spirituality lies right here—that there is a barrier of unacknowledged sin between modern Christians and God, an estrangement which makes prayer impossible.

Sin and the confession of sin are now unpopular subjects in the church. The penitential elements in the liturgical services have been greatly reduced. The pendulum has swung from too much expressed contrition to none at all. In churches such as the Roman Catholic and Anglican, where sacramental confession has been practiced, this ministry has shrunk so drastically that it seems to be disappearing.

The reasons for all this are various. An over-emphasis on sin in the neo-orthodoxy of the tragic years of depression and war, a legalistic concept of sin in the pre-renewal days of the Roman Church, the substitution of psychiatric for pastoral approaches to guilt—all of these have their part to play in the phenomenon. But most basically, the loss of the sense of sin comes from the loss of the sense of a God who is holy and righteous, "unto whom all hearts are open, all desires known, and from whom no secrets are hid."

A loss of a sense of sin does not mean the end of the reality of sin. Sin is like a sickness: a man may not know he is sick and yet be sick; a man may not want to face the fact that he is sick and yet die of his sickness. There is every reason to believe that our society is full of unadmitted problems of unresolved guilt. This condition has invaded the church. Before we can pray again, we may need the realism of the way of confession: "have mercy on me, a sinner."

The purpose of confession of sin is not to induce depression, but to obtain forgiveness. So often we become fixated on the profoundly penitential expressions of the liturgical forms that we forget that they are followed by *absolution.*

Kyrie eleison, as treated by Bach in the *Mass in B Minor,* and in its original meaning, is not a cry of sorrow, but a shout of joy. The Lord always does have mercy. The Prayer of Jesus is simply claiming constantly the unremittingly-offered redemption of Christ.

The source of forgiveness is the life, death, and resurrection of Jesus made present by the power of the Holy Spirit. Confession of sin is not a dismal outcry; it is being brought to Christ to be healed by him. It is the joy of restoration, release, and freedom. But it costs something.

Forgiveness does not come by the good-natured nod of

God. Paul saw that, Anselm saw that, Luther saw that, Wesley saw that, Barth saw that—Christians in every century have seen that forgiveness comes because God did something about sin. What he did can be seen as sacrifice, a taking upon himself of the guilt of the world in Jesus. The holy and righteous God loves us in this costly way and removes the barrier between ourselves and him to make our prayer possible. God has already acted in Calvary and the resurrection. All he requires is that we take the responsibility for our sin and keep turning back, keep relating to Christ in trust. This makes the reconciliation by the union which comes from at-one-ment. This is the experience of salvation by faith which is the ground of all prayer.

The Prayer of Jesus is only one instance of the practice of praying continually. It serves a purpose for many Christians of the West because it has the surprise of a new discovery. There is nothing especially Eastern about praying constantly.

After preaching on this subject in a cathedral, I was talking with a retired bishop who had achieved deserved fame as a distinguished administrator. He remarked that he could never see why "praying without ceasing" was considered so unusual; he himself had assumed that Christians should pray about what they were doing while they were doing it, and that he had done this all his life.

When this kind of praying has become instilled within a believer, he begins to sense that something is happening in him. His prayer prays in him, to use the Pilgrim's phrase. To put it in the language of Paul, he realizes that he is "praying in the Spirit." There is a real similarity between the Prayer of Jesus and glossolalia. Both are forms of praying in which the pray-er finds himself filled with the action of God. Any such experience destroys all sense of the unreality of prayer. No longer does it seem like talking to yourself, or speaking to someone unhearing at a great distance, for it is something which happens in you, not just something that you do.

Paul gropes for words, writing in his letter to the Romans as he seeks to phrase this experience: "We do not even know how we ought to pray, but through our inarticulate groans the Spirit himself is pleading for us, and God who searches our inmost being knows what the Spirit means, because he pleads for God's people in God's own way" (Romans 8:26-27). In the letter to the Ephesians Paul puts this more buoyantly: "Give yourselves wholly to prayer and entreaty; pray on every occasion in the power of the Spirit. To this end keep watch and persevere, always interceding for all God's people: and pray for me, that I may be granted the right words when I open my mouth, and may boldly and freely make known his hidden purpose, for which I am an ambassador—in chains. Pray that I may speak of it boldly, as it is my duty to speak" (Ephesians 6:18-20).

When a believer comes into this experience, then, and perhaps, only then, can he make sense of the question of petition and intercession: What can we pray for? The answer is simple—anything and everything that a son can ask of a loving Father, for by the power of the Spirit we can ask in union with his Son who is our brother.

Christian believing leads into being-in-Christ in prayer. If Jesus is Lord we are dealing with a living person, and it is only natural that our relationship with him becomes a kind of continual conversation. This passes into an inner union of heart and very self which is expressed whenever we call him by his name: "Jesus."

CHAPTER IX

Coming to the End

The End of it all has broken into the midst in Jesus Christ! This is the ground of Christian hope. All that Christian believing projects about the final destiny of man, the world, and all there is, comes from the resurrection of Jesus of Nazareth.

The last book of the Bible, the Revelation of St. John the Divine, excites the reader with a great swirling mass of images of the final judgment, like a painting of Marc Chagall, with vision superimposed upon vision. It belongs to a kind of literature which is nowhere written now, called apocalyptic, a vivid and sometimes terrifying work of imagination about what finally shall be. That sort of composition did not enjoy long life in Christian communication, but it served a purpose. The book of Revelation is not, as some people have believed, a literal description of heaven or some kind of foretelling of future events in history, but a great and glorious phantasm of the final triumph of Christ. The important thing to remember is that it was composed to strengthen the church in Rome during the deadly persecution of Domitian.

At the beginning of the book is the first vision of the Triumphant Christ who announces the meaning of it all:

He laid his right hand upon me and said, "Do not be afraid. I am tne first and the last, and I am the living one; for I was dead and now I am alive for everyone, and I hold the keys of Death and Death's domain. Write down therefore what you have seen, what is now, and what will be hereafter." (Revelation 1:17-19)

This is the pattern. Christ is risen from the dead. This has the inevitable consequence that in him is the secret, the secret of what is, and what is to be. Christian faith does not expect or give any answers about the future or eternity or the end of the world that cannot be found in the person of Christ—that cannot be found in him as a *person*. It might be put this way: the eschatology of Christian faith is the "therefore" of the resurrection of Christ.

The word "eschatology" is necessary for an understanding of what we are talking about. It comes from the Greek word *eschaton,* which means "end." It is not the kind of end to be found in the end of a string, or at the end of one's rope—a terminus. It is the kind of end which we think of when we say, "What end do you have in mind," or, "With this end in view. . . ." It is a purposeful end, a fulfillment, or perhaps best of all, a consummation. When Christians speak of Christ as "the Alpha and the Omega," "the Beginning and the End," we mean that Christ is the consummation.

Such a faith comes from the startling impossibility of a man being raised from the dead. The resurrection of Jesus, whom we know and love, was a triumph over the total malignancy of evil which concentrated upon him and destroyed his life. The cross and the awfulness of the lostness of the Son of God in his death become the ground of hope. He has won over the uttermost. Since he has thus destroyed the final power of evil, *therefore* "he is destined to reign until God has put all enemies under his feet. . ." (I Corinthians 15:26). This is the "therefore" of Christian hope, the "therefore" of Christian eschatology.

Such a vision of the Lordship of Christ is a vision of Christ as Judge. This concept comes from the teaching of Jesus himself, but it excites abhorrence in many people. When the notion has been made too dominant, as in certain times in the Middle Ages, the need for mercy has developed a whole cult of intermediaries between God and man in the form of interceding saints. This is a serious aberration, but equally bad is the idea that God tolerates all kinds of evil, that he is so "loving" that he could never have wrath, and that Jesus is in no sense Judge at all.

When Jesus taught of the last judgment and of hell, he taught it as an aspect of love. Those who were unloving, who did not see Christ in the needy, are condemned. The love that God reveals in Jesus is real and active, and has consequences. This does not mean that we make the judgment; but he does. It does not mean that we know who is judged; but he does. It does mean that damnation is a possibility for me, because he never coerces me to love. That I know full well. Believing that Christ is Judge simply means meeting the living Christ, having to come to terms with the living Christ, who demands love—forgiving love.

One of the strangest phenomena in the church today is the loss of the sense of divine judgment at the very moment we undertake with special urgency the changing of society. When the prophets spoke against injustice, they did so in the name of a just God who requires it. They saw that God's justice can be discerned even in the rough justice of history. When Jesus denouced the evil of his time, he spoke fearsome words of warning of ultimate responsibility. Those who follow in the prophetic tradition which Jesus fulfilled have always done the same. Sometimes, alone against terrible power, they have effected change because they conveyed a sense of God's own imperative. One of the reasons why the present church has not been able to sustain motivation for projects for social change lies in the fact that it has taken its impulse from secular society rather than from the prophetic tradition. There cannot be real Christian social action without eschatology.

The Christian conception of the End is cosmic; it is of the universe, of all that is. A tremendous need for a sense of cosmic meaning has erupted in our culture. A new feeling for the unity of the cosmos and our involvement in it springs from modern developments. Space travel has shattered our earthbound provincialism. The threat of the destruction of the earth by pollution produced the ecological concern which has become practically a religion. The great mobility of multitudes has brought us all in touch with cultures and histories very unlike our own, who have a deeper sense of the unity of the whole of creation. The breakdown of meaning has made it apparent that to survive in a technological world we have to have answers about all reality as well as questions, answers which include everything. How many people seek a satisfaction for this need in something like the mysteries of Tibet without realizing that the greatest cosmic awareness can be found in Christian faith itself!

The Christian attitude toward the cosmos comes from the resurrection of Christ's body. God does not just raise the spirit of Christ from the dead, but all there is of him. This means that the redemption which God effects in Jesus pertains not only to the things of the spirit but to materiality as well. The resurrected body of Christ is transformed for this purpose.

The transfiguration of the world is the concept of the cosmic consummation in the New Testament. Eastern Christians have perceived this better than Western Christians. There is an exciting ancient and modern literature about this which we can well study. The transfiguration of Christ is the precedent for this hope.

The story of the transfiguration of Jesus has to do with his resurrection; in fact, some scholars have prematurely suggested that it is a misplaced resurrection appearance. It looks instead like the supreme instance of the phenomenon of "mystic light" which has been recorded of many saintly persons who in a state of peculiar unity with the divine "light up." [21] In the Gospel narrative this comes as a sequel to Jesus telling his disciples that he must go to Jerusalem to be crucified, and that they must follow his way of the cross (see Mark 8:30–9:10). The context is Jesus' acceptance of the inevitability of his death. That is the moment—not a moment of mystical rapture—that the glory shines through. The light penetrates the body of Christ, and even "his clothes became dazzling white, with a whiteness no bleacher on earth could equal" (Mark 9:3). That detail of the garments expresses the way the early church understood the total significance of the moment: it involved all that Christ touched, materially as well as spiritually. For an instant the veil was taken away and his disciples saw him, uncomprehending, for what he is. Eastern theology speaks of the transfiguration of Christ as the vision of the uncreated Light, of the transfusion of Christ with the energies of God. This arresting language conveys the meaning. The transfiguration is the pattern of what Christ is for, what the death and the resurrection are for—cosmically. It is the pattern of the purpose of God—to fill all things with himself through Christ.

The first chapter of the Epistle to the Colossians affirms this cosmic expectation. The writer, Paul or some other, develops this theme in a great prose hymn about Christ:

He rescued us from the domain of darkness and brought us away into the kingdom of his dear Son, in whom our release is secured and our sins forgiven. He is the image of the invisible God; his is the primacy over all created things. In him everything in heaven and on earth was created, not only things visible but also the invisible orders of thrones, sovereignties, authorities, and powers: the whole universe has been created through him and for him. And he exists before everything, and all things are held together in him. He is, moreover, the head of the body, the church. He is its origin, the first to return from the dead, to be in all things alone supreme. For in him the complete being of God, by God's own choice, came to dwell. Through him God chose to reconcile the whole universe to himself, making peace through the shedding of his blood upon the cross—to reconcile all things, whether on earth or in heaven, through him alone. (Colossians 1:13-20)

At first it may seem that the hope of Christ filling and fulfilling all things is a dreamy mystic vision which quiets the believer with a cosmic glow. Far from it! The Christian hope comes on a man as a moral imperative. It means that God's concern and God's redemption have to do with all things, not just personal salvation and religion alone. This destroys the compartmentalization of life for a Christian, with spiritual matters sequestered in one compartment. Faith has to do with all that there is, with the world as God made it, and as he shall consummate it. If this is God's intent, it has to be ours now, for every one of us has to face his ultimate future as part of that consummation.

We live in the meantime: in the meantime between the now and the then, between the now of our knowledge of God's purpose and the then of its fulfillment. And in this meantime we are responsible for making our hope come true. What God has revealed in the vision of what the world is for, is what is potential but unrealized in creation and history. This becomes a call to action, to realize this potential through the power of Christ now. Therefore, the practical consequence for Christian hope is the changing of ourselves and the world, the materiality and the spirituality of the world, the individuality and the society of the world, here and now, by the power of the resurrection in us so that the End keeps breaking into our midst.

The Theologians of Hope have made a great contribution at this time in showing the way in which Christian eschatology, the Future of Jesus Christ as Lord of all, must motivate Christians in their engagement with every cause which promotes human justice and freedom. A Christian finds in this ultimate hope a theology of history and of action which can have revolutionary consequences for society. Cosmic glory has to do with politics, aesthetics, education, economics, sex—all things, both here and hereafter, now and then.

Our personal destiny, eternal life, must be considered only in this context. How easy it is to focus on our own urgent anxiety about survival after death, and never get the full Christian answer because we are so self-centered. Our destiny is to be a part of it all. Every individual is known, loved, and redeemed for all eternity as himself, but at the same time as part of *it all*.

This has to do with death, but with more than death. Everyone who reads this book knows he has to die, but we try to put away this knowledge. Facing death is particularly difficult for Americans. Our cult of the dead with its pathetic and bizarre efforts to avoid the reality of death betrays this fact. Even Christians become infected with this disease of unreality about death. They can show it by pretending that there is something beneath their consideration in the question of life after death. This is not a Christian reaction. A Christian can face death, not because of something noble about himself, but because he knows that "the life of the world to come" is what he is made for and redeemed for, both now and in the cosmic consummation. It was bought with a price by Jesus the Lord.

William Laud, Archbishop of Canterbury and Martyr of the seventeenth century, uttered this strange and wonderful prayer on the scaffold:

Lord, I am coming as fast as I can. I know I must pass through the shadow of death, before I can come to thee. But it is but *umbra mortis,* a mere shadow of death, a little darkness upon nature: but thou, by thy merits and passion, has broken through the jaws of death. So, Lord, receive my soul, and have mercy upon me. . . . [22]

"Lord, I am coming as fast as I can"—this is the Christian believer's way of death and way of life. This comes from the understanding of our relationship to Jesus Christ which is phrased in the First Epistle of St. John: "We are God's children now; it does not yet appear what we shall be, but we know that when he appears we shall be like him, for we shall see him as he is" (I John 3:2, RSV). Taking these words phrase by phrase, we can enter into the Christian understanding of the End to which we come:

We are God's children now. Eternity is now; the experience of Jesus Christ who is the End of it all begins now. We are dealing with a Presence. He is knowable in the joy of meeting him in the Breaking of Bread, in continuing prayer, and in the constant pressure of his urging, his judging, his forgiving, and his strengthening of our wills. The ground of our expectation is not a theory or a memory, but an encounter that is constantly going on. The result of this is an awareness that, because of our relationship to his Son, God accepts us as his sons; we are thereby his children *now.*

It does not yet appear what we shall be. There is always an agnosticism about eternal life for the Christian. He is not told exactly "what it will be like." He is given no map of heaven, no description of the process of resurrection, or the nature of his resurrection body, or the resurrection body of the world. This is not an anxiety, but the joyful expectation of divine surprise.

We know that when he appears we shall be like him. This is what we know. We know that nothing is going to get lost, because Christ is all there in his resurrection. The principle of "like him" is the shape of our own fulfillment. Our resurrection is like his; our union with God, like his, because his Incarnation is God's gift to us. This union is of such intensity that it means being incorporated through him into the very life of God, into the society of awful love which is the Trinity of God; but *incorporated,* embodied—not disembodied, but embodied—in some way whereby all that we ever were or shall be is transfigured "like him."

For we shall see him as he is. This is the End. The End of it all is Christ. It is a meeting with Someone we know, with Someone we have expected, or perhaps more truly, Someone who has expected us, Someone who has gone before.

Christian believing turns an expectation into a vocation. Jesus Christ who is the End of it all calls us and the world to himself. In a decisive way, this happens finally at his "Second Coming" at our death and the world's death. In a constant way, it occurs in the decisions of life when we must come after him, not shrinking to deny ourselves, to take up our cross, and follow him, through death to resurrection. The life of a Christian believer is always a coming to the End, and there is the urgency of meeting Christ in every moment of it—"Lord I am coming as fast as I can."

Notes

1. "The Jesus of History" in G.K.A. Bell and D.A. Deissmann, *Mysterium Christi, Christological Studies by British and German Theologians,* Longmans, Green, London, 1930, pp. 31-33, italics mine.
2. Ibid., p. 32, italics original.
3. Ibid., p. 34, italics original.
4. D.M. Baillie, *God Was in Christ: An Essay on Incarnation and Atonement,* Charles Scribner's Sons, New York, 1948, 45-46.
5. *The Hymnal 1940,* Church Hymnal Corp., New York, #63.
6. Ibid., #66.
7. *The English Hymnal,* London #130.
8. *The Hymnal 1940,* #91.
9. Sir Edwyn Hoskyns, "The Christ of the Synoptic Gospels," in *Essays Catholic and Critical,* E.G. Selwyn, ed., SPCK, London, 1926, p. 151.
10. See John Austin Baker, *The Foolishness of God,* Morehouse-Barlow Co., New York, 1970, pp. 157-158.
11. Julien Green, *Diary 1928-1957,* selected by Kurt Wolff, tr. Anne Green. Harcourt Brace Jovanovich, New York, 1964, p. 202.
12. Malcolm Muggeridge and Alec Vidler, *Paul, Envoy Extraordinary,* Harper and Row, New York, 1972, pp. 11-13.
13. Quoted in Romano Guardini, *Pascal for Our Time,* Herder and Herder, New York, 1966, pp. 33-34. Used with the permission of the McGraw-Hill Book Co.
14. Note: I am indebted to the Rt. Rev. Alan Clark, Roman Catholic Bishop of Elham, England, for stimulating this insight in a lecture at Trinity Institute.
15. Quoted by Timothy Ware in *The Orthodox Church,* Penguin Books, London and Baltimore, 1963, p. 73.
16. Note: The earlier works of Bonhoeffer, which he wrote while immersed in community, such as *The Cost of Discipleship,* do not contain this problem. It should also be remembered that even in prison Bonhoeffer himself was a "religious" man, praying, preaching, celebrating the Christian festivals, and recalling the ceremonies of Holy Week in Rome. A recent documentation of the false diagnosis of the inevitably secularized future can be found in Andrew Greeley's *Unsecular Man* (Schocken Books, New York, 1972). This volume was reviewed in *The New York Times* on two successive days because of its important.
17. Timothy Ware, *op. cit.,* p. 216.
18. *The Emergence of the Catholic Tradition,* Vol. 1 of *The Christian Tradition* University of Chicago Press, Chicago and London, 1971, p. 1.
19. Harcourt Brace, New York and London, 1971.
20. Seabury Press, New York, 1965.
21. See Timothy Ware, The Transfiguration of the Body," in *Sacrament and Image,* Fellowship of St. Alban and St. Sergius, London, 1967 and Mircea Eliade, "Experiences of the Mystic Light," *Images and Symbols,* Sheed and Ward, New York, 1963.
22. Quoted in E. Milner-White and G.W. Briggs, compilers, *Daily Prayer,* Pelican Books, Hammondsworth, Middlesex, 1959, p. 187.